PHP 7

An Object Oriented Design Patterns Study

Sanjib Sinha

This book is for sale at http://leanpub.com/php7in7days

This version was published on 2017-03-28

Leanpub

This is a Leanpub book. Leanpub empowers authors and publishers with the Lean Publishing process. Lean Publishing is the act of publishing an in-progress ebook using lightweight tools and many iterations to get reader feedback, pivot until you have the right book and build traction once you do.

To Arun Sengupta

Remembering the golden working days we had worked together...

Contents

CONTENTS

CONTENTS

Note from Author

This book is an Introduction to Design Patterns and Object Oriented Programming with an Overview of the New Features of PHP 7: Scalar type declarations, Return type declarations, Null coalescing operator, Spaceship operator, Constant arrays using define(), Anonymous classes, Closure::call(), Group use declarations and many moreâ€¦

Cover Design

Kaberi Sinha

Graphic Art and Typography

Amitakkhar Deb

About the cover photograph

This photo was taken in Chitor, Rajasthan, nearly ten years back.

Until that time the outskirt of Rajasthan, the town famous for forts, had been lonesome and blue.

When you walked along the ruins you feel sorry for the common people, farmers, workers and artisans who once had to sacrifice their lives fighting for protecting the properties of the kings.

What makes PHP 7 so special?

The very first thing is of course speed. It's been found by the developers, around the world, php 7 is twice as fast as 5.6 and in some cases it's faster! Since it's tested on widely used php CMS like wordpress and drupal, you can bet on it.

The founder developers have been working hard on this issue since long time. Speed really matters and the developers always want one thing. The language code-base should reduce memory consumption and increase performance.

Php 7 has touched that dream. ...

Who should read this book?

This book is intended for everyone. From an absolute beginner to a seasoned php developers who frequently use procedural methods but have never tried OOP seriously.

Besides, for absolute beginners I have written a quick recapitulation that will guide you to the php core concepts.

How to upgrade to PHP 7

I presume you're running php 5.x on an Ubuntu 14.04 machine. If you're windows based, you can easily install Ubuntu 14.04 as a second operating system.

Remember, a genuine php programmer should know a little bit of Linux programming. It's extremely easy and user friendly. Install Ubuntu on your system and open the terminal by pressing 'control+alt+t'. For further association with Linux there are tons of free resources available over the internet.

You've opened up your terminal; now type this command on it.

```
1   sudo add-apt-repository ppa:ondrej/php
```

A Personal Package Archive, or PPA, is an Apt repository hosted on Launchpad. PPAs allow third-party developers so that they can build and distribute packages for Ubuntu outside of the official channels. They're often useful sources of beta software – php 7 is also on the developmental stage and it's not ready for the production environment.

Ondřej Surý maintains the PHP packages for Debian (Ubuntu uses a Debian version), and offers a PPA for PHP 7.0 on Ubuntu. As a beginner you may find this concept little bit difficult to follow. But, don't worry. You'll get acquainted with it in coming times.

Once the PPA is installed, update your local cache to get the contents with this command.

```
1   sudo apt-get update
```

It'll take some time to update and ask for more space to install php 7 packages. Once it's done, you can check your php version with a simple command.

```
1   php -v
```

It'll give a nice output that will confirm that you have php 7 installed on your system.

```
1  PHP 7.0.10-2+deb.sury.org~trusty+1 (cli) ( NTS )
2  Copyright (c) 1997-2016 The PHP Group
3  Zend Engine v3.0.0, Copyright (c) 1998-2016 Zend Technologies
4      with Zend OPcache v7.0.10-2+deb.sury.org~trusty+1, Copyright (c) 1999-2016, \
5  by Zend Technologies
```

You have php 7. Now you can keep your php code anywhere in your machine. For local development you may place your codes in '/var/www/html' folder. But it's not mandatory that you should always keep your codes there.

I make a directory in my 'home' folder just by issuing a simple command on the terminal.

```
1  mkdir Code
```

A 'Code' folder has just been generated. Let us create another folder 'php7book1' inside it. We are about to create our further php 7 project in this folder so first of all we should check whether our php 7 is working perfectly. To do that, we must run the local server first. Next, we'll open up our browser and type http://localhost:8000 so that a php info page will be opened up.

How did I do this?

The very first step was, I created an 'index.php' page inside 'php7book1' folder and I wrote the simple 'phpinfo()' function inside it.

```
1  //Code/php7book1/index.php
2  <?php
3  echo phpinfo();
```

To run the local server, we need to issue this command. But you have to stay inside your project folder.

```
1  php -S localhost:8000
```

Once this command has been issued, you can open your browser and type http://localhost:8000. When your local php server is running, the terminal starts giving you these commands.

```
1  PHP 7.0.10-2+deb.sury.org~trusty+1 Development Server started at Thu Sep 15 09:4\
2  0:44 2016
3  Listening on http://localhost:8000
4  Document root is /home/hagudu/Code/php7book1
5  Press Ctrl-C to quit.
6  [Thu Sep 15 09:41:00 2016] 127.0.0.1:37991 [200]: /
7  [Thu Sep 15 09:41:01 2016] 127.0.0.1:37992 [404]: /favicon.ico - No such file or\
8   directory
```

...

Now you're ready to start your first day. Remember, it's our mission to complete our journey in seven days. Within that limit we will have a quick recapitulation on php variables, functions, object oriented programming and design patterns. Our final segment includes a looking up to the cool features of php 7. ...

Day 1

We have planned to finish our study within seven days. This stipulation may seem difficult.

And it's really difficult.

You can never learn a programming language within seven days. It may take more than seven years to master it. I don't want to claim that I'll teach php 7 in seven days.

Then how can this book help you to achieve your goal of learning php 7?

First of all, I can give you few fundamental ideas about the features of php 7. Along with I can help you get a solid understanding of object oriented programming (OOP). From there you can take forward your further studies on php. I genuinely hope it helps.

And to do that you must remain focused for seven days and follow the guide exactly as it goes.

In the first chapter we'll learn the basics of object oriented programming and php 7. In the second chapter we'll go for a very quick and short-lived recapitulation. We'll learn type summery, php functions and writing simple classes.

From this point we'll start climbing the mountain slowly. First come namespace, trait and json. These concepts are absolutely necessary for the further study.

In the php world there has been a silent revolution taking place with "Composer". We'll learn what is composer. How it works. How we can work with other classes using composer.

In the last section of we discuss about solid design principle.

It's not difficult at all. Once you understand this concept OOP and coding will be much simpler and a real fun.

Let's move!

OOP and PHP 7

For absolute beginners, the term OOP or Object Oriented Programming may seem difficult. Some people want to mystify this term very heavily! Why? Because, the uninitiated PHP developers would never try to make their hands dirty and feet wet with code and will depend on them forever.

So the first step is start believing in your potentials, powers and strength of your mind. Coding is like writing. I show you how easy it is!

Consider a piece of writing where you're trying to describe a robot. So in your writing 'robot' is the subject. In object oriented programming the 'robot' is the object. In your piece of writing, your subject 'robot' has some descriptions like – the robot has three eyes, two noses, six arms.

In OOP we need to write a class 'Robot' which has those properties like this:

```php
//Code/php7book1/index.php
<?php
class Robot {
    public $eye;
    public $nose;
    public $arm;
    public function showRobot($eyes, $noses, $arms) {
        $this->arm = $arms;
        $this->eye = $eyes;
        $this->nose = $noses;
        echo "The robot has {$eyes} eyes, {$noses} noses, {$arms} arms";
    }
}
//class ended
$robot = new Robot();
$robot->showRobot(3, 2, 6);
```

When you run this script, the output is as expected: The robot has 3 eyes, 2 noses, 6 arms.

All we have done is very simple – we wrote a Robot class where we have defined properties and methods. Next, we have created a robot object and through which we have put some life into it. The robot has jumped into life and says it has 3 eyes, 2 noses and 6 arms.

Is it okay? Apparently, it's definitely okay. But, there could be some problems. Suppose somebody changes the last line of code.

```
1    $robot->showRobot(3, two, 6);
```

Look, instead of passing an integer the user passes a string. Well, php will tackle it by its own way. It'll give you an output like this: The robot has 3 eyes, two noses, 6 arms.

But, we intended to give an integer, isn't it?

In PHP 7 this problem has been solved. The scalar type declaration has made it mandatory to pass integer when integer value has been asked for.

Let us write our old code this way.

```
1    //Code/php7book1/index.php
2    <?php
3    class Robot {
4        public $eye;
5        public $nose;
6        public $arm;
7        public function showRobot(int $eyes, int $noses, int $arms) {
8            $this->arm = $arms;
9            $this->eye = $eyes;
10           $this->nose = $noses;
11           echo "The robot has {$eyes} eyes, {$noses} noses, {$arms} arms";
12       }
13    }
14    //class ended
15    $robot = new Robot();
16    $robot->showRobot(3, 2, 6);
```

The change has taken place only on this line:

```
1    public function showRobot(int $eyes, int $noses, int $arms)
```

Here we have mentioned, categorically, that the parameters should be passed as integers. Now, if anybody passes string or any thing other than integer it'll throw errors.

A Quick Recapitulation

We store information in variables. Since php 7, you need not 'type hint' the variable and you can pass any value through any variable – integer, string, double (floating point number), Boolean or NULL. PHP has been very forgiving in that sense.

You can always write a variable like this:

```
1   $variable = 'some string values';
```

So you need a dollar sign before and a '=' operator after so that a variable denotes a value. The value of a variable is always the recently assigned value. Like I first wrote:

```
1   $variable = 'some string values';
```

If I change to this:

```
1   $variable = 10;
```

The value of '$variable' is now 10. In php 7 when we assign an integer value, we write like this:

```
1   int $variable = 10;
```

Now you try to change it to some string value, it'll throw an error.

Type Summery

PHP has altogether eight types: integer, doubles, string, Booleans, arrays, NULS, objects, and resources.

To Remember

Integer is a whole number like 132.

Doubles are floating point number like 123.562438 or 48.0.

Strings are sequences of characters like 'I have a dream.'

Booleans have only two possible values: TRUE and FALSE.

Nulls are a special type that has only value NULL.

Arrays are named and indexed collection of other values.

Objects are instances of user-defined classes as we have just seen in case of Robot class. It has all properties and methods that one or more related classes contain. We'll see it in detail later.

Resources are variables that contain references to other resources external to PHP like MySQL database connection.

PHP Function

It's the action part of your programming. In OOP it's often called methods. The first major advantage of a function is that you can actually reuse it any time and as many time. A simple example shows a function with one parameter.

```
1   function functionName($param) {
2       return $param;
3   }
```

A parameter is usually referenced as an argument also. As you see, a function has four parts. A special type word 'function', comes first then comes the name of the function. You must make a function name understandable. You can pass parameters or arguments with a '$' sign attached to it. The final part is the body of the function where you define the action part. You can use all the logical part of your programming inside the body of the function.

More about Functions ...

Function lies in the heart of php programming. Usually a piece of code is encapsulated inside a function, so that it can be called whenever you need it. In that sense, a function is invaluable.

Remember never start a function name with a number. It is not case sensitive. Underscore is widely used. Some people prefer to call it method. So function and method is same. Both mean to 'do something'. In object oriented programming we will come to this topic once more and see how it really means to 'doing something'!

Let us do something with our function.

```
1        function hello()
2        {
3            echo "hello everyone";
4        }
5        //now call this function
6        hello();
7        //done, it will echo  hello everyone.
8
9    Every function in PHP returns value. Whether you explicitly force it to return a\
10    value or not, it'll always return values.
11
12        function hello($you)
13        {
14            echo "I love {$you}";
15            if ($you == "12reach"){
16        return;
17    //nothing has been processed
18                }
19                echo ", what about you?";
20        }
21            //now call this function
22            hello("12reach");
23    // Displays I love 12reach
24            hello("PHP"); // Displays I love PHP, what about you?
```

Variable scope is very important. You may use $_GLOBAL super global array.

```
1        $a = "Hello";
2        $b = "Everyone";
3        function hello()
4        {
5            global $a, $b;
6            echo "$a $b";
7        }
8        hello(); // Displays "Hello Everyone
9
10    You may write it this way.
11
12        $a = "Hello";
13        $b = "Everyone";
14        function hello()        {
15        echo $GLOBALS['a'] .' '.
```

```
16      $GLOBALS['b']
17      }
18      hello(); // Displays "Hello Everyone"
```

You can create a function that accepts variable number of arguments. And it is extremely useful.

```
1   function reach() {
2   if (func_num_args ()>0){
3       $arg = func_get_arg(1);
4       echo "You want to reach {$arg}";
5   }
6   else {
7           echo "12reach is want to reach!";
8       }
9   }
10  reach("12reach", ", or somewhere else?");
11  //Output is: You want to reach, or somewhere else?
12      reach();
13  //Output is: 12reach is want to reach!
```

Summery of Simple Classes

Let us first see a simple piece of code.

You have already learned about OOP. We just try to take that knowledge a bit further and add some juice into it.

We are imagining about a "Car class". We want to make several new cars from it with different features. Next we'll try to discuss about the advantages and limitations of using these new car objects.

Let us see the code first:

```
1   <?php
2
3   class Car {
4       public $color;
5       public $is_bought = false;
6
7       public function __construct($color) {
8           $this->color = $color;
9       }
10
11      public function buy() {
```

```
12              $this->is_bought = TRUE;
13      }
14  }
15
16  $suzuki = new Car("RED");
17  var_dump($suzuki->color);
18  var_dump($suzuki->is_bought);
```

Run it either on your browser or on the terminal. You'll get this output:

```
1  string(3) "RED"
2  bool(false)
```

It says the new car object "suzuki" is of red color. Then we ask, "Is it bought?" The default value is 'false' so it comes out as "bool(false)". Let us create another car object "maruti" and let it call the "buy()" method.

Look at the code.

```
1  public function buy() {
2              $this->is_bought = TRUE;
3      }
```

The "buy()" method makes the property "is_bought" – TRUE.

```
1  $maruti = new Car("Blue");
2  var_dump($maruti);
3  $maruti->buy();
4  var_dump($maruti->is_bought);
```

So when we create another car object "maruti" we get this output.

```
1  object(Car)#2 (2) {
2    ["color"]=>
3    string(4) "Blue"
4    ["is_bought"]=>
5    bool(false)
6  }
7  bool(true)
```

You see the code now becomes more meaningful and close to the reality. It's not that everybody goes to the car showroom to buy a car. For that reason we have kept the "is_bought" property "false". When the consumer buys a car it sets to "TRUE".

This scenario changes when two developers from two different parts of the world work on the same "Car class". Suppose they both name their file "car.php". A name collision is inevitable. What you can do to avoid such unpleasant situation?

The answer is "Namespace".

Namespace, TRAIT and JSON

What is Namespace?

Well, the name suggests it, I guess. It's great news for developers as it is a great relief for them. They don't have to write unnecessary long name of methods to avoid name collisions.

As you know, 'foo.txt' can not appear in the same directory. You have to place them in a separate directory like '/home/ss/folderone' and '/home/ss/foldetwo' and finally when you call 'foo.txt' from a certain folder, you need to mention the whole path. Using the directory separator you can only reach '/home/ss/folderone/foo.txt' and the same rule is applicable for the other folders also.

In PHP world, 'namespace' serves the same purpose and many more. It avoids name collision encapsulating items. Namespaces are designed to solve the problem in the same way as authors of libraries and applications can write the reusable codes without worrying about the name collisions. Now they can write short classes and functions.

Let us see some examples and make it clear. Before we go through an example there is one important thing to remember. In PHP 5 or higher version through namespace only classes (abstract classes and traits), interfaces, functions and constants are affected.

```php
1   <?php
2   namespace MyProject\sub\level;
3   const CONNECT_OK = 1;
4   class Connection { ... }
5   function connect() {....}
6   ?>
```

Declaring multiple namespaces in a single file is permissible but not desirable. In PHP 7, we'll see later, how this problem has been solved.

It is a good practice to separate them: like in 'secondExample.php' we use:

```
1   <?php namespace English\Grammar;
2    include 'past.php';
3    class Tense {
4       protected $verb;
5        public function continuous($example) {
6            $this›verb = $example;
7            return $example;
8        }
9   }
10  //unqualified name
11  $obj1 = new Tense;
12  echo $obj1›continuous('test present'); //output test present
13  echo "<br›";
14  //qualified name
15  $obj2 = new Past\Tense();
16  echo $obj2›continuous('test past');
17  //output test past
```

And in another file, say its name is 'thirdExample.php', we use the same class and function's name like below:

```
1   <?php namespace English\Grammar\Past;
2   class Tense {
3       public $verb;
4       public function continuous($example) {
5            $this›verb = $example;
6            return $example;
7        }
8   }
```

You see in 'secondExample.php' that there is a hierarchy maintaining throughout the code. In 'thirdExample.php' file we use this:

```
1   namespace English\Grammar;
2   And in 'thirdExample.php' we use this:
3   namespace English\Grammar\Past;
```

It is obvious from two files that 'thirdExample.php' lies one level deep. When we include that in 'secondExample.php', it is obvious that we need not mention the full path. We could have done that and in that case, it would have been a fully qualified path.

So we in 'secondExample.php' we use the level deep path and call the class and function like this:

```
1   $obj2 = new Past\Tense();
2   echo $obj2>continuous('test past'); //output test past
```

The example is fairly simple but in nature complex enough to solve a big problem of name collisions. In your namespace you can use any class, interface, function or constant without worrying about the name collisions.

Suppose you have a namespace 'Myname'. You have another namespace 'Yourname' and in that namespace you have a class 'YourClass'. Now we can write it like this:

```
1   namespace Myname;
2   use Yourname\Yourclass as Darling;
3   $obj = new Darling();
```

Now we can extend this property more and organize our application further and build a library. Just like this:

```
1   <?php
2   namespace MyBlog;
3   use YourBlog\YourBlog as Darling;
4   use HisBlog\HisBlog
5   use HerBlog\HerBlog
6   use TheirBlog\TeirBlog as Blog
7   ...
```

Want to extend it further? You can organize your post, content, category like this:

```
1   <?php
2   namespace MyBloq;
3   use YourBlog\YourBlog\content\page
4   use YourBlog\YourBlog\content\post
5   use YourBlog\YourBlog\category
```

I hope now it makes sense. Namespace does not stand for only name conflict but it is a weapon of organizing your files. And that you can use in your applications.

How to Autoload Namespace?

After the 'Composer' revolution in php world the whole environment has changed a lot. Now auto loading namespace seems to be a child's play.

Using 'composer.json' file we can also avoid writing the long namespace reference. That is a great advantage now.

Suppose, you have an application named 'PHP7BOOK'. Now you want to keep your all folders in the 'source' folder.

One line in 'composer.json' file is enough.

```
1  {
2      "autoload": {
3          "psr-4": {
4              "PHP7BOOK\\": "source"
5          }
6      }
7  }
```

You have not learned 'Composer' yet. So this code might look indecipherable.

By the next chapter you'll have learned about 'Composer'. And in chapter 12 you will get the feel about architecture design. In that chapter you'll also learn about autoloading namespace through 'Composer'. It's closely related to the architecture design of your application.

What is Trait?

First let's discuss about Traits. This feature is a recent inclusion in PHP world. It is available from php 5.4.0 and basically used for code reuse. In that sense, it has a similarity with namespace; but it is entirely different. PHP is a single inheritance language. It is widely useful here. You can use it inside the class like this:

```php
1  <?php
2  trait TraitReflectionReturnInfo {
3      function getReturnType() { /*1*/ }
4      function getReturnDescription() { /*2*/ }
5  }
6  class TraitReflectionMethod extends
7  ReflectionMethod {
8      use TraitReflectionReturnInfo;
9      /* ... */
10  }
11  class TraitReflectionFunction extends
12  ReflectionFunction {
13      use TraitReflectionReturnInfo;
14      /* ... */
15  }
```

This is nothing but an addition to the traditional inheritance. How this inheritance works will be clearer from this example:

```php
1   <?php
2   class BaseClass {
3       public function Hello() {
4           echo 'PHP ';
5       }
6   }
7   trait MyWorld {
8       public function Hello() {
9           parent::Hello();
10          echo '7 Learner.';
11      }
12  }
13  class MyHelloWorld extends BaseClass {
14      use MyWorld;
15  }
16  $object = new MyHelloWorld();
17  $object>Hello();
18  ?>
19  // The output will be 'PHP 7 Learner'.
```

The advantageous code reuse opened up new avenue in the PHP world. Remember one thing, code reuse was the major headache in PHP which has been solved by these features. Another great thing is 'Composer'.

It is a package manager that will take care of almost everything. It has changed the way PHP world worked before. How?

You have already listened about dependency injection and you will be hearing it lot in the future. Composer has made this job much easier than one can imagine. Composer is a JSON file.

What is JSON?

Since version 5.2.0 PHP has started serialize and unserialize data in JSON format. Let's see how it looks:

```php
1   $book = array('Words'=>'Jean Paul Sartre');
2   echo json_encode($book);
```

It has got an output like this:

```
1   {"Words":"Jean Paul Sartre"}
```

But if we want to reverse the procedure, there is a little trick and json_decode() function has some other tricks in its possession.

Now you can realize the power of JSON. Not only it can be used for data transaction but you can also use it as flat file configuration. And that has what exactly been done by Composer.

Since composer has come up, you need not create namespace file manually. Composer will look after it. Besides, through 'composer.json' you can always update your project. Moreover, you can also auto load every file at one go. Composer has many advantages that you have not had before. It makes PHP developer's life much easier.

Composer Revolution

Composer is a dependency management tool in PHP. For any PHP project you need to use your library of codes. Composer easily manages that task on your behalf helping you to declare those codes. You can also install or update any code in your library through composer. Please visit https://getcomposer.org for more details.

In the opening page of https://getcomposer.org, click the 'getting started' link.

In the above page you find two links – 'locally' and 'globally'. It stands for two options. Suppose you don't want to run composer globally or centrally in your system. In that case, you have to download and install composer each time for every project. But the global option is always preferable because once composer is installed in your system bin folder you can call it anytime for any project.

If you are already accustomed with any Linux distribution like Ubuntu you know that for any local PHP project we use to go to '/Code/php7book1' folder. Suppose we are going to build a simple PHP project and we want to name it 'php7book1'. Open up your Ubuntu terminal (control+alt+t) and first go to that folder first.

To reach there you need to type the following command on your terminal:

```
1   cd Code/php7book1/
```

Once you've reached, you can make a directory here with a simple command:

```
1   sudo mkdir php7book1
```

It will ask for your 'root' user password. Type the password and a folder called 'php7book1' will be created.

Next in this folder we'll download and install 'composer'. Considering you are a beginner, for the sake of brevity I want to download and install composer locally on our Laravel project.

Next issue these two commands – one after another. First you type:

```
1   sudo php -r "copy('https://getcomposer.org/installer', 'composer-setup.php');"
```

It'll take some time. Next type this:

```
1   sudo php composer-setup.php
```

It'll organize your composer setup file to go further. Actually your composer is ready to download packages for your coming project. You can test it by creating a 'composer.json' file inside your folder. In that 'composer.json' file type this:

```
1   {
2       "require": {
3           "monolog/monolog": "1.0.*"
4       }
5   }
```

What does this mean? It means you're installing 'monolog' PHP package for your Laravel project. Will it come to any immediate use? The answer is 'NO'. We're actually testing our composer installer and want to see how it works.

Now you can issue the command that will install 'monolog' package for you. Type this command on your terminal:

```
1   php composer.phar install
```

It'll take a little time to install the 'monolog' package. It depends on your internet speed.

After the installation is over you'll find a 'vendor' folder and few 'composer' files inside your project. Feel free to discover what is inside the 'vendor' folder. There you'll find two folders – 'composer' and 'monolog'. Again you can see what they have inside them. As a beginner it's an endless journey to discover new things. Try to get acquainted with everything new you have found.

The time has come to install Laravel 5.2 through composer. You can install Laravel just like monolog. It means, you can write that instruction in your 'composer.json' file and just update your composer. But as a beginner I recommend to follow the simple-most method. ...

SOLID Design Principle

Let us see what this SOLID design principle is. This book is not a place to put forward a detail description of SOLID principle. But at least we can discuss about this principle in a nutshell.

SOLID design principle is the five principles articulated by Robert "Uncle Bob" Martin that consist of five principles. In a nutshell I am going to tell them one by one. In the final part I will discuss it in detail.

SOLID stands for

Single Responsibility Principle

Open Closed Principle

Liskov Substitution Principle

Interface Segregation Principle

Dependency Inversion Principle

The Single Responsibility Principle means a class should have one and 'only one' reason to change. Knowledge about the class should not be open. The class' scope should be narrowly focused. A class would do its job and not at all be affected by the change that takes place on its dependencies. Remember if we can build a library of small classes with well defined responsibilities our code will be more decoupled and easy to test and run.

Open Closed Principle means a class is always open for extension but closed for modification. What is that?

It states that change the behavior without modification of source codes. If you can do your job without touching the source code, it's always better! Remember what Uncle Bob says, "Separate extensible behavior behind an interface and flip the dependencies." The thing is anytime you modify your code there is a possibility to break the old functionalities completely adding new bugs. But if you can plan your application in the beginning based on Open Closed Principle, you could modify your code base as quickly as possible without getting affected.

What is Liskov Substitution Principle?

Don't get frightened. This looks intimidating, but as a principle it is extremely helpful and easy to understand. It says: Derived classes must be substitutable for their based class. It means objects should be replaceable with instances of their subtypes without altering the correctness of program. If you can not follow it for the present moment, please move on, I will explain these principles in detail with examples screenshot so that the picture will be much clearer. What is Interface Segregation Principle?

It is nothing but an echo of Singular Responsibilities. If it is broken, Singular Responsibility is broken. In a nutshell it says: interface should be granular and focused. No implementation of interface should be forced on methods that it does not use. Accordingly break into small interfaces as you require them for your implementation. Plan it before and enjoy the decoupled easy going ride.

Finally, here comes the Dependency Inversion Principle.

It states that high-level codes should not depend on low-level codes. Instead the high-level code depends on 'Abstraction' that plays a middle man between high-level and low-level. The second aspect is abstraction does not depend upon details but details depend upon abstractions.

For the beginners these principles may look uncomfortable but don't worry. When we will discuss it in detail with examples you'll see it's very simple and helpful to understand object oriented programming and its design patterns. You have already found the term 'Interface' and 'Abstraction' more than once.

Interfaces and Method Injection

Abstraction in OOP involves extraction of relevant details. Consider the role of a car salesman. There are many types of consumers. Everyone wants to buy a car, no doubt, but each one has his or her own differences in their criteria. Each of them is interested in one or two certain features.

This attribute varies accordingly. Shape, color, engine power, power steering, price ... the list is endless. The salesman knows all the details of the car but does he repeat the list one by one until someone finds his or her choice? No. He presents only the relevant information to the potential customer. As a result the salesman practices 'Abstraction' and presents only relevant details to the customer.

Now consider abstraction from the perspective of a programmer who wants a user to add items to list. Abstraction does not mean that information is unavailable or kept secret but it assures that the relevant information is provided to the user.

PHP 5 introduces abstract classes and methods and in PHP 7 it improves a lot. In the PHP 7 features section we'll see them in detail.

Classes defined as abstract may not be instantiated and any class that contains at least one abstract method must also be abstract. Remember abstract methods can not define the implementation. On the other hand, object interfaces allow you to create code which specifies which methods a class must implement, without having to define how these methods are handled.

Interfaces are defined with the interface keyword, in the same way as a standard class, but without any of the methods having their contents defined. All methods declared in an interface must be public; this is the nature of an interface. We'll see lots of examples of this SOLID design principle in the coming chapters.

Day 2

The second day has many things for us in its store.

First we'll look after the overview of classes and objects. We'll learn how together how to use getter and setter methods and why they are needed?

The second part of the day is extremely essential. We'll learn about abstraction and encapsulation. Interface or contract plays a very important role in our endeavor to achieve maximum performance.

Let us start our second day with overview of classes and objects.

Overview of Classes and Objects

A class is a blueprint. A plan of doing something. Suppose we want to keep reviews through a class. Objects contain data and methods to send and receive messages.

It decides how a 'review' object will behave in future. Every object may not behave in the same fashion because one review may remain incomplete. You've to think every possibility before planning a class. It's a good practice to have your pen and notebook ready so that you can write it down completely. What you're going to do will be your flow chart. And the code you write inside your class will be your algorithm.

Now we have a 'Review' class.

We've decided to keep three properties. Category, title and content. Whenever we create an object or instance of this class, these three properties will be passed through the constructor method. Next we wanted to add one more property. We name this property 'complete'. By default we set this property value 'FALSE'.

Only when the 'review' object hit the 'complete' method, this property will change to 'TRUE'. Let us view the code first.

```php
1    //Day2/review.php
2    <?php
3    class Review {
4        public $category;
5        public $title;
6        public $content;
7        public $complete = false;
8
9        public function __construct(
10               $category = 'Category to be filled up.',
11               $title = 'Title to be filled up.',
12               $content = 'Content to be filled up.'
13               )
14       {
15           $this->category = $category;
16           $this->title = $title;
17           $this->content = $content;
18           echo $category . "=" . $title . "=" . $content;
19       }
20
```

```
21            public function completed() {
22                $this->complete = TRUE;
23                echo '....Review Completed';
24            }
25
26            public function notCompleted() {
27                echo $this->complete . '....Review Not Completed';
28            }
29    }
30
31      $review1 = new Review('Cinema', 'The Enemy of the State',
32                'A very good movie. It is full of action and drama.');
33      $review1->completed();
34      echo '<br>';
35      var_dump($review1);
36      echo '<br>';
37      $review2 = new Review('Cinema', 'The Edge');
38      $review2->notCompleted();
39      echo '<br>';
40      var_dump($review2);
```

In the code section it's clear that we set the properties first. Next we set two methods. We have also created two instances of the class 'Review'.

The first instance calls the 'complete' method. But the second instance or review object is not complete. Let us have a more detail introspection of this class 'Review'. Whenever an instance or object is created, the constructor method is called. For that reason we decided to pass the arguments through it. Those arguments or parameters may contain the value. We wanted to write simple reviews, where a category, a title will be kept up with the body content. We'd also like to mention whether our review is completed or not completed.

The logic is simple and the algorithm is not very complex. Look at the separation of the code. The first object does not get affected when the second object remains incomplete.

The advantage and strength of Object Oriented Programming lie here. You can keep everything separated and loosely coupled. Imagine the functioning of the car parts. If your horn does not work it'll not affect any other part. If you want to stop the car, apply the brake and you can stop it. Our code is also telling about that separation.

Now we'll see the output of our code first.

```
1   //the first object
2   Cinema=The Enemy of the State=A very good movie. It is full of action and drama.\
3   ....Review Completed
4   object(Review)#1 (4) { ["category"]=> string(6) "Cinema" ["title"]=> string(22) \
5   "The Enemy of the State" ["content"]=>     string(50) "A very good movie. It is \
6   full of action and drama." ["complete"]=> bool(true) }
7   //the second object
8   Cinema=The Edge=Content to be filled up.....Review Not Completed
9   object(Review)#2 (4) { ["category"]=> string(6) "Cinema" ["title"]=> string(8) "\
10  The Edge" ["content"]=> string(24)              "Content to be filled up." ["complete\
11  "]=> bool(false) }
```

From the output it's clear that what we wanted at the very beginning finally ends up successfully.

What you can do?

You can add one more property to this class. Name it 'rating'. Since you're coding in PHP 7, you can keep that property 'integer'. Try to pass any other value than integer and watch the errors. ...

Get, Set and Go...

In any class the properties play very roles. Till now we use 'public' before every property. In the real world the situation may not be same.

Imagine an 'Instrument' class. In the construct part you can pass the name of the instrument. Besides, you can have a property – 'weight'. Let us write the code first and see the output.

```
1   //Day2/instrument.php
2   <?php
3
4   class Instrument {
5       public $name;
6       public $weight;
7       public function __construct($name) {
8           $this->name = $name;
9       }
10  }
11
12  $guiter = new Instrument('Elictric Guiter');
13  $guiter->weight = 10;
```

If we use 'var_dump($guiter)' we know what will be the output.

```
1   object(Instrument)#1 (2) { ["name"]=> string(15) "Elictric Guiter" ["weight"]=> \
2   int(10) }
```

Now consider a situation where the weight of the guiter should be less than 2 KG. The logic is simple. We set the weight first and then get the output. In the 'set' function we may use 'if-else' logic. There is no problem in doing that. Let's try.

```php
1    <?php
2
3    class Instrument {
4        public $name;
5        public $weight;
6        public function __construct($name) {
7            $this->name = $name;
8        }
9        public function getWeight() {
10           return $this->weight;
11       }
12       public function setWeight($weight) {
13           if ($weight > 2){
14               throw new Exception('The weight is not permissible.');
15           }
16           $this->weight = $weight;
17       }
18   }
19
20   $guiter = new Instrument('Elictric Guiter');
21   $guiter->setWeight(30);
22   var_dump($guiter->getWeight());
```

It promptly throws the fatal error.

```
1    PHP Fatal error:  Uncaught Exception: The weight is not permissible. in /home/ha\
2    gudu/Code/php7book1/Day2/instrument.php:20
3    Stack trace:
4    #0 /home/hagudu/Code/php7book1/Day2/instrument.php(28): Instrument->setWeight(30)
5    #1 {main}
6      thrown in /home/hagudu/Code/php7book1/Day2/instrument.php on line 20
```

Using this logic we're still in danger. Since the property 'weight' is 'public' it still can be accessed directly. Whatever precaution we take may not come to our use, unless we change the 'access modifier' of the property which is 'public'.

The question of hiding our business logic from public gaze comes to our mind. The idea of encapsulation also comes handy in such cases. In the next chapter we'll deal with that.

Hiding Information

There was a hole in the previous code.

Did you notice that?

Let us examine this part of code:

```
1  $guiter = new Instrument('Elictric Guiter');
2  $guiter->setWeight(1);
3  $guiter->getWeight();
4  $guiter->weight = 10;
5  var_dump($guiter);
```

And the output is simply mind blowing.

```
1  object(Instrument)#1 (2) {
2    ["name"]=>
3    string(15) "Elictric Guiter"
4    ["weight"]=>
5    int(10)
6  }
```

Look, we set the weight of the instrument to less than 2 KGs – we've set it to 1 – but in the final output the weight has come up as 10.

How did it happen?

It's happened, because, in the last line of code we have directly call the 'weight' property and assign a value which is greater than 2 KGs. It was simply pathetic. Our entire efforts of making 'setter' and 'getter' functions to restrict the weight less than 2 KGs just have vanished into blue. It was overwritten simply by one 'access modifier' – 'public'.

If we had made it 'private' it could not have been accessed so easily. Let us see what output comes out by changing the entire code.

```
1   <?php
2
3   class Instrument {
4       private $name;
5       private $weight;
6       public function __construct($name) {
7           $this->name = $name;
8       }
9       public function getWeight() {
10          return $this->weight;
11      }
12      public function setWeight($weight) {
13          if ($weight > 2){
14              throw new Exception;
15          }
16          $this->weight = $weight;
17      }
18  }
19  $guiter = new Instrument('Elictric Guiter');
20  $guiter->setWeight(1);
21  $guiter->getWeight();
22  $guiter->weight = 10;
23  var_dump($guiter);
```

Here is the output.

```
1   PHP Fatal error:  Uncaught Error: Cannot access private property Instrument::$we\
2   ight in /home/hagudu/Code/php7book1/Day2/instrument.php:23
3   Stack trace:
4   #0 {main}
5     thrown in /home/hagudu/Code/php7book1/Day2/instrument.php on line 23
```

It's worked finally. It cannot access the private property. It was what we wanted. One word – 'private' makes things worse for the unwanted assessors.

Now imagine your home. Not every room should be accessible by the strangers who come to meet you. May be you invite that person to your sitting room. Your bed room is either protected or private.

Let us consider a class 'Room' and test our code.

```php
1  <?php
2
3  class Home {
4      private $name;
5      private $color;
6      public function __construct($name) {
7          $this->name = $name;
8      }
9      public function getColor() {
10         return $this->color;
11     }
12     public function setColor($color) {
13         if ($color == 'black'){
14             throw new Exception;
15         }
16         $this->color = $color;
17     }
18     private function moveToBedroom() {
19         return "Restricted";
20     }
21 }
22 $home = new Home('Castle of the Heavens');
23 $home->setColor('white');
24 $home->getColor();
25 var_dump($home);
```

The output is quite expected.

```
1  object(Home)#1 (2) {
2    ["name":"Home":private]=>
3    string(21) "Castle of the Heavens"
4    ["color":"Home":private]=>
5    string(5) "white"
6  }
```

You have noticed that there is a private method. Now we're going to access that method just by adding this line to our code (marked in red).

```
1  $home = new Home('Castle of the Heavens');
2  $home->setColor('white');
3  $home->getColor();
4  $home->moveToBedroom();
5  var_dump($home);
```

The output is utterly different from the previous one.

```
1  PHP Fatal error:  Uncaught Error: Call to private method Home::moveToBedroom() f\
2  rom context '' in /home/hagudu/Code/php7book1/Day2/home.php:28
3  Stack trace:
4  #0 {main}
5    thrown in /home/hagudu/Code/php7book1/Day2/home.php on line 28
```

As we progress we'll find more examples of such encapsulations. When you write your class, you must know what properties should be made public or what should be private. There is another 'access modifier', called 'protected'. In the next chapter we'll see how that works.

Inheritance, Encapsulation, Abstract Class and Interface

In Dictionary if you search the word 'inheritance', you'd land up finding this kind of description: ...objects that someone gives you when they die.

In the programming world, it does not mean exactly the same in every sense but almost same if you take the literal meaning. Yes, there is a parent class with one or more child classes who inherit the objects from their parents but child classes are freer here, in the php programming world. These child classes are free to modify or override the properties and methods that they inherit. In real world it does not happen always.

Let us a have a simple code to check a parent class and child class.

```php
1    //Day2/inheritance.php
2    <?php
3    //parent class Instrument
4    class Instrument {
5        protected $name;
6        protected $weight;
7        public function __construct($name) {
8            $this->name = $name;
9        }
10       public function getWeight() {
11           return $this->weight;
12       }
13       public function setWeight($weight) {
14           if ($weight > 2){
15               throw new Exception;
16           }
17           $this->weight = $weight;
18       }
19   }
20   //child class Guitar
21   class Guitar extends Instrument {
22   }
23   $guitar = new Guitar('Electric Guitar');
24   $guitar->setWeight(1);
25   $guitar->getWeight();
26   var_dump($guitar);
```

The output is as expected.

```
1  object(Guitar)#1 (2) {
2    ["name":protected]=>
3    string(15) "Electric Guitar"
4    ["weight":protected]=>
5    int(1)
6  }
```

The child class 'Guitar' has inherited each property from its parent class 'Instrument'. When you create a guitar instance it automatically inherits every property.

This situation may not persist all along. We could have many child classes all together that inherit the properties and methods of the parent class but want to behave on their own way. Everyone wants freedom, isn't it?

In such cases, a 'Spanish Guitar' class may not agree with the weight of an 'Electric Guitar' class. A Spanish guitar may want to be lighter than an Electric guitar. In such case a child class should have an ability to override the methods of the parent class that have a definite algorithm to set the weight. Let us see how we can solve this problem.

```php
1  //Day2/instrument.php
2  <?php
3  class Instrument {
4      protected $name;
5      protected $weight;
6      public function __construct($name) {
7          $this->name - $name;
8      }
9      public function getWeight() {
10          return $this->weight;
11      }
12      public function setWeight($weight) {
13          if ($weight > 2){
14              throw new Exception;
15          }
16          $this->weight = $weight;
17      }
18  }
19  class SpanishGuitar extends Instrument {
20
21      public function getWeight() {
22          return $this->weight;
```

```
23        }
24        public function setWeight($weight) {
25            if ($weight > 2){
26                throw new Exception;
27            }
28            $this->weight = $weight;
29        }
30    }
31    class ElectricGuitar extends Instrument {
32
33        public function getWeight() {
34            return $this->weight;
35        }
36        public function setWeight($weight) {
37            if ($weight > 10){
38                throw new Exception;
39            }
40            $this->weight = $weight;
41        }
42    }
43    $spanish_guitar = new SpanishGuitar('Spanish Guitar');
44    $spanish_guitar->setWeight(1);
45    $spanish_guitar->getWeight();
46    var_dump($spanish_guitar);
47    $electric_guitar = new ElectricGuitar('Electric Guitar');
48    $electric_guitar->setWeight(8);
49    $electric_guitar->getWeight();
50    var_dump($electric_guitar);
```

Let us first run this code and see the output.

```
1    object(SpanishGuitar)#1 (2) {
2      ["name":protected]=>
3      string(14) "Spanish Guitar"
4      ["weight":protected]=>
5      int(1)
6    }
7    object(ElectricGuitar)#2 (2) {
8      ["name":protected]=>
9      string(15) "Electric Guitar"
10     ["weight":protected]=>
11     int(8)
12   }
```

As expected. In our code, we have two child classes – Spanish Guitar and Electric Guitar. Each one has its own weight criteria. A Spanish Guitar should come out lighter than an Electric Guitar. Hence, the algorithm changes inside them. They just override their respective parent method.

Introducing Abstraction and Encapsulation

These two features are very important for any object oriented programming language. Abstraction involves extracting only the relevant information. Encapsulation means packaging one or more two components together.

Defining Abstraction

A car salesman always gives relevant information to a potential customer. He knows that different people have different preferences. Keeping that in mind he only presents and stresses specific feature to a potential customer. Although all customers want to buy a car bur some of them consider the price first, some search for a specific color, some are interested on engine and speed – actually each of them has a specific point of interest. A good salesman always follows that trend and presents only the relevant part.

This is the core concept of abstraction or abstract classes. The information is hidden but not unavailable. All information exist but only the relevant ones are presented.

Defining encapsulation

Encapsulation literally means 'enclosing some information in a capsule or package'. For example when we switch on the car engine, we do not see the complex processes going on inside the bonnet. How battery, fuel, engine work together remains encapsulated. We can, for that reason, say that encapsulation is also explained as data hiding or information hiding.

Difference between Abstraction and Encapsulation

They are different but related. You encapsulate information into a package and abstraction enables you to present relevant information from that package.

Abstract Classes

Considering the previous codes we have used before, we're still not contented with this design pattern because, as you see in the code, we had to overuse our methods extensively. It is working fine, no problem, but we want more flexibility in our code. Consider this code.

```php
//Day2/abstract_instrument.php
<?php
abstract class Instrument {
    protected $name;
    protected $weight;
    public function __construct($name = 'Guitar') {
        $this->name = $name;
        return $this->name;
    }
    public function getWeight() {
        return $this->weight;
    }
    public function setWeightforSpanish($weight) {
        if ($weight > 2){
            throw new Exception;
        }
        $this->weight = $weight;
    }
    public function setWeightforElectric($weight) {
        if ($weight > 10){
            throw new Exception;
        }
        $this->weight = $weight;
    }
}
class SpanishGuitar extends Instrument {
}
class ElectricGuitar extends Instrument {
}
$spanish_guitar = new SpanishGuitar('Spanish Guitar');
$spanish_guitar->setWeightforSpanish(2);
$spanish_guitar->getWeight();
var_dump($spanish_guitar);
```

```
34   $electric_guitar = new ElectricGuitar('Electric Guitar');
35   $electric_guitar->setWeightforElectric(8);
36   $electric_guitar->getWeight();
37   var_dump($electric_guitar);
```

The previous code had 49 lines of code. And the modified version of that code has got 37 lines. We are able to reduce 12 lines of code and at the same time we also make our codes more readable and modular. The only difference is we declared our parent class abstract. What the heck is it?

Imagine something abstract that transcends into the child classes as the lineage. Exactly same thing happens here. We can even modify our child classes by adding more methods to it.

Let's change that part and see the output.

```
1    class SpanishGuitar extends Instrument {
2        public function run() {
3            echo "You don't need electric.";
4        }
5    }
6    class ElectricGuitar extends Instrument {
7        public function run() {
8            echo "You need electric.";
9        }
10   }
11   $spanish_guitar = now SpanishGuitar('Spanish Guitar');
12   $spanish_guitar->setWeightforSpanish(2);
13   $spanish_guitar->getWeight();
14   $spanish_guitar->run();
15   var_dump($spanish_guitar);
16   $electric_guitar = new ElectricGuitar('Electric Guitar');
17   $electric_guitar->setWeightforElectric(8);
18   $electric_guitar->getWeight();
19   $electric_guitar->run();
20   var_dump($electric_guitar);
```

The output is like this.

```
1   You don't need electric.object(SpanishGuitar)#1 (2) {
2     ["name":protected]=>
3     string(14) "Spanish Guitar"
4     ["weight":protected]=>
5     int(2)
6   }
7   You need electric.object(ElectricGuitar)#2 (2) {
8     ["name":protected]=>
9     string(15) "Electric Guitar"
10    ["weight":protected]=>
11    int(8)
12  }
```

The only problem of an abstract class is that, it does not support instantiation and its method should not be left empty. To overcome this difficulty the concept of interface has come up as huge help.

Basic Interfaces

Interfaces are also called contracts. It actually defines the syntactical contract that all the derived classes should follow. Let us consider an example first to understand how this contract works.

```
1   interface InputOrderDetails {
2       public function UpdateCustomerStatus();
3       public function TakeOrder();
4   }
5   class ItemDetails implements InputOrderDetails {
6       public function UpdateCustomerStatus(){
7           var_dump("Updating customer...");
8       }
9       public function TakeOrder(){
10          var_dump("Taking orders..");
11      }
12  }
13  $item1 = new ItemDetails;
14  $item1->TakeOrder();
15  $item1->UpdateCustomerStatus();
```

We have an interface which defines a syntactical contract and the class follows those contracts exactly as it has been defined.

Look at the output.

```
1   string(15) "Taking orders.."
2   string(20) "Updating customer..."
```

Now we can move forward this contract to furthermore. We can imagine a situation where we can use our interface concept to hide information. Consider the contract between the seller companies a buyer. The buyer does not know how the product reaches to her. Besides, the seller also does not want to accept the responsibility of carrying the product on its own to the house of the buyer. So the company gives that responsibility to a courier company. Now the courier receives the product from the seller and carries to the buyer.

In this scenario, the courier does not know what type of product it's carrying to the buyer. We follow the SOLID Design principle exactly as we have wished to do.

Let us see the code, it tells a relationship and messaging between many objects.

```php
1   <?php
2   interface Deliverer {
3       public function deliver($user);
4   }
5   class Retailer implements Deliverer {
6       public function deliver($user) {
7           var_dump("One book sent to..." . $user);
8       }
9   }
10  class User {
11      public $deliverer;
12      public function __construct(Deliverer $deliverer) {
13          $this->deliverer = $deliverer;
14      }
15      public function recieve() {
16          $user = "Sanjib";
17          $this->deliverer->deliver($user);
18      }
19  }
20
21  $user = new User(new Retailer());
22  $user->recieve();
```

The 'Retailer' delivers the instruction to the 'Deliverer'. So there is a contract between them and the retailer needs user as a parameter to whom it will send the item. Retailer knows the nature of the item, what item it's sending; but deliverer doesn't know about it. The deliverer only delivers and does not know anything. The buyer only receives, so she needs one 'deliverer object' who will deliver. Exactly the same thing happens here. Look at the code and the output below.

```
1  string(25) "One book sent to...Sanjib"
```

Day 3

Our third day consists of four chapters – first we'll get an overall idea about Design Patterns, and after that we'll learn to use strategy pattern.

Next we'll learn more about Architecture and finally Factory Patterns will come up.

What is Design Pattern

Sometimes a web application may be very simple and based on a typical single request and response process. Sometimes it can be very complex.

You may think of an E-Commerce project or a social media platform where the design of the application needs to be complex and several developers have to work on it.

The question is how would you like to structure the code? It's very important to plan it earlier. There are several reasons for doing that.

The main reason is: your code of any type of web applications may involve other developers. They should be able to understand what you're writing. It couldn't be puzzling. It should be simple and elegant so that one can understand and work on it.

Keeping that reason in mind, you can either put a lot of thought into it – developing your own design – or you can follow the common patterns.

Developing your own style has always been a very encouraging idea but to do that you need to know what has been done before. Following common patterns is a good idea for the beginners. You need some time to develop your skill as a competent php developer. Before that study the common patterns and follow them so that others can also understand your code.

Here we'll look into some of the common patterns.

One of them is "Factory Pattern". It is one of the most frequently used patterns in the history of php coding. In object oriented programming (OOP), a factory pattern is primarily an object that creates other objects. A class simply creates an object and the process moves on.

Another pattern is "Singleton". The meaning is quite literary. Singleton means one and only. When a class is not allowed to instantiate more than one object, the pattern is known as singleton. Sometimes it's useful. Sometimes you need one, just one object that will coordinate actions across the system. It's come from the mathematical concept of singleton.

One of the very popular approach or pattern is MVC or Model-View-Controller pattern. In this pattern controller handles the request and process the data coming from model and load the views to send in the response. This pattern lets you break the code into logical objects that serve very specific purpose.

MVC is the most common architectural pattern used in the popular PHP framework.

Another pattern you very often use in your applications. It is 'front controller' pattern. In this pattern you have a single entrance point (index.php) that handles all the requests coming to your application.

In a typical case of an online purchase it handles all the tasks like session handling, caching etc. The front controller code is responsible fro loading all of the dependencies. After loading the dependencies it processes the request and sends response to the browser. It's the central place that supports modular coding. Besides, every code should run through it.

The alternative to the front controller might be breaking your codes to various other scripts like log in page or registration page.

There are many more patterns and in the coming chapters we'll look into few of them. We'll start with strategy pattern. It's also called policy pattern.

What is Your Strategy?

Strategy pattern is a set of patterns that involve few interchangeable algorithms in a family of code. These algorithms not only interchange in the run time but also encapsulate themselves so the client classes don't know what is happening inside.

You have already known about the encapsulation and interface. You have learned about the contract. Strategy pattern tells about the same thing.

Let us experiment with a code so the conception will be much clearer. Consider a code snippet where we have three separate algorithms of validating name, password and age. It's impossible to hard code them each time. Instead we can make it interchangeable in the run time so that we don't need to think about it each time.

To do that we encapsulate those algorithms through a contract so that client class doesn't know what's happening inside.

First we see the hard coding part where we have not implemented strategy pattern.

```php
1   <?php
2   class ValidateAge {
3       public function validate($param) {
4           var_dump("Validating age.");
5       }
6   }
7
8   class ValidateName {
9       public function validate($param) {
10          var_dump("Validating name.");
11      }
12  }
13
14  class ValidatePassword {
15      public function validate($param) {
16          var_dump("Validating password.");
17      }
18  }
19  class Application {
20      public function validate($param) {
21          $validator = new ValidateAge();
22          $validator->validate($param);
```

```
23        }
24  }
25  $application = new Application();
26  $application->validate("Some information");
```

You see through our application object we hard coded some information. There is no interface or contract and no implementation either.

There are three algorithms and each time you need to validate you have to hard code the client class.

Let us open our terminal and run this code to see how it works.

```
1  hagudu@hagudu-H81M-S1:~/Code/php7book1/Day3$ php strategy.php
2  string(15) "Validating age."
```

It's working. But there is nothing new in it.

Each time you need to validate some algorithm, you have to hard code them. Moreover your client class also knows which algorithm you're using. This strictly violates our SOLID principle.

To rectify that fault we can make a policy pattern or change our strategy.

Consider this code.

```php
1  <?php
2  interface Validate {
3      public function validate($param);
4  }
5
6  class ValidateAge implements Validate {
7      public function validate($param) {
8          var_dump("Validating age.");
9      }
10 }
11
12 class ValidateName implements Validate {
13     public function validate($param) {
14         var_dump("Validating name.");
15     }
16 }
17
18 class ValidatePassword implements Validate {
19     public function validate($param) {
20         var_dump("Validating password.");
21     }
```

```
22  }
23  class Application {
24      public function validate($param, Validate $validator) {
25          $validator->validate($param);
26      }
27  }
28  $application = new Application();
29  $application->validate("Some information", new ValidatePassword);
```

In this new strategy we have used a contract "Validate" which simply validate data. We're doing that by passing a parameter. Now in each algorithm we implement that contract and finally in the run time we just change the name.

In our code we use "ValidatePassword". We could have used "ValidateAge" or "ValidateName". No matter. It'll work. Let us see the output:

```
1  hagudu@hagudu-H81M-S1:~/Code/php7book1/Day3$ php strategy.php
2  string(20) "Validating password."
```

Now we change the last line of this code using different class algorithm this time. We want to validate name.

```
1  $application = new Application();
2  $application->validate("Some information", new ValidateName);
```

Let us see the output:

```
1  hagudu@hagudu-H81M-S1:~/Code/php7book1/Day3$ php strategy.php
2  string(16) "Validating name."
```

It's working and while working our client class doesn't know the name of the class algorithm because until run time because it has been encapsulated. In the run time we supply the name and it executes validation without knowing what's happening behind. We can select the algorithm's behavior at runtime and that's our strategy.

So we can say the strategy pattern defines a family of algorithms first and then encapsulates each algorithm in the second step, and finally makes the algorithms interchangeable within our code family.

In the real world the validation processes will definitely be different.

Validating age will never be same as validating password. But the class which is performing validation on incoming data (here our Application class) is actually using a policy or strategy pattern to select the validation algorithm based on the type of the data.

For each case you see that these factors are not known until run time. When we select the validation name (age, name or password) in the last line of code only then it knows and accordingly different algorithm is performed.

More about Architecture

You have got an idea of design pattern in the previous chapter where you have seen how 'strategy pattern' works. How you have to plan the design. How you need to design the pattern.

Before digging deep into other design patterns you'd better learn the core architecture first. After that we can move on learning other design patterns.

In object oriented programming a class is treated as a part of a larger blueprint. There could be three or four classes or there could be hundreds and thousands. It depends on what are you going to make. Before making something you need to plan it well before. Architecture deals with those core issues.

The main purpose of architecture is setting an environment where objects can pass messages between themselves so that your application runs smooth.

Let us start with a small example. Imagine a dictionary. Suppose you're to build up an application where users can add new words and their meanings. While creating such application you have to keep one thing in your mind. Your app should follow 'SOLID' principle. The objects should be loosely coupled.

The second thing that you need to keep in mind is: how first object pushes the second object to do something that will ultimately affect the third object. It's a kind of a messaging system where first object sends message to the second one and the second object finally passes the message to the third object.

As the size of your application grows, the number of classes and activities of objects grow along with it. Let us start with our mini app 'dictionary', where we add a word with its meaning and place it into the dictionary. Finally we get the output.

To plan such architecture what do you need first?

We need a 'Word' class. After that we need a 'Dictionary' class that would add words. But there is a glitch. In a dictionary only words are not supposed to be added. You need to define that word with a meaning.

So we need a 'Meaning' class.

** Things are developing now. **

If we want to write the whole thing in simple English we'll write something: a dictionary object would add word. It'll be a method that would call upon a method where a meaning object would use a define method where the meaning of the added words would be defined.

We'd write this process inside a 'add' method like this in the dictionary class:

```
1     public function add(Word $words) {
2         $this->meaning->define($words);
3     }
```

And to facilitate our effort we also need to create a 'Meaning' class. As you see, the whole process involves three classes:

1) Word

2) Dictionary

3) Meaning

In 'Word' class we'll only define the word property. It has no other functions. The 'Dictionary' class needs to have an 'add' method where the words will be added. Inside the 'add' method we'd like to use 'Meaning' object that'd use a 'define' method to define the meaning of the words.

This is our structure.

Once the structure of the application has been set, you can move on writing the classes and methods. Let us see the code how it looks like.

```php
1   <?php
2
3   class Word {
4
5       protected $words;
6
7       public function __construct($words) {
8           $this->words = $words;
9       }
10  }
11
12  class Dictionary {
13
14      protected $meaning;
15
16      public function __construct(Meaning $meaning) {
17          $this->meaning = $meaning;
18      }
19
20      public function add(Word $words) {
21          $this->meaning->define($words);
22      }
23
24  }
```

```
25
26  class Meaning {
27
28      protected $definitions = [];
29
30      public function define(Word $words) {
31          $this->definitions[] = $words;
32      }
33  }
34
35  $meaning = new Meaning();
36  $dictionary = new Dictionary($meaning);
37
38  $a = new Word("The Noun 'a' has seven senses.");
39  $dictionary->add($a);
40  $meander = new Word("to move or cause to move in a spiral way.");
41  $dictionary->add($meander);
42  var_dump($meaning);
```

Before we try to understand the code by dissecting the lines, you'd prefer to see the output.

```
1   object(Meaning)#1 (1) {
2     ["definitions":protected]=>
3     array(2) {
4       [0]=>
5       object(Word)#3 (1) {
6         ["words":protected]=>
7         string(30) "The Noun 'a' has seven senses."
8       }
9       [1]=>
10      object(Word)#4 (1) {
11        ["words":protected]=>
12        string(41) "to move or cause to move in a spiral way."
13      }
14    }
15  }
```

Let's slice up the code. The very first object we need is 'word'. For that we have written a 'Word' class.

```
1   class Word {
2
3       protected $words;
4       public function __construct($words) {
5           $this->words = $words;
6       }
7   }
```

There is nothing special in it. Through constructor we'll pass the meaning of the word. Next we write 'Dictionary' class.

```
1   class Dictionary {
2
3       protected $meaning;
4
5       public function __construct(Meaning $meaning) {
6           $this->meaning = $meaning;
7       }
8
9       public function add(Word $words) {
10          $this->meaning->define($words);
11      }
12
13  }
```

Through the constructor method we have passed the 'meaning' object. And later in the 'add' method the 'meaning' object has used 'define' method by passing the 'word' object as its parameter.

Now all you need to write a 'Meaning' class where you can write the 'define' method.

```
1   class Meaning {
2
3       protected $definitions = [];
4
5       public function define(Word $words) {
6           $this->definitions[] = $words;
7       }
8   }
```

In future we may want to add many definitions to our words. For that reason we wanted our definition property to iterate.

As you find, there is nothing special in it.

The later part of the code is self explanatory. We have created a 'meaning' object first. Then we create a 'dictionary' object.

```
1   $meaning = new Meaning();
2
3   $dictionary = new Dictionary($meaning);
4
5   $a = new Word("The Noun 'a' has seven senses.");
6   $dictionary->add($a);
7   $meander = new Word("to move or cause to move in a spiral way.");
8   $dictionary->add($meander);
9
10  var_dump($meaning);
```

So far we've written the whole code in a single file. But we need to keep them in separate files and through one entry point we'd run our whole application. So that when user runs the application the objects pass messages between them from different sources and make the app run successfully.

In the next chapter you'll learn how it can be done.

12.1 – Compose the Architecture

In the last chapter we've worked with a single file where we kept three classes – Word, Dictionary and Meaning. We created objects from each classes and saw how the objects passed messages between them and ran the application in a synchronized way.

In real world, this doesn't happen. Once you've decided to create an application, one thing you should keep in your mind. Several developers may take part in your project. What is more, they might take part from distant parts of the world. They should be able to work at tandem in a synchronized way.

Imagine a situation where your main three classes – Word, Dictionary and Meaning – are staying at one folder. Let us name it 'sources'.

If you want to run this app using the procedural way, you'd probably use the default php 'require' function to add the files on the top of the index file.

But, does it sound good for the other developers who have been working at tandem with you for this application? You're smart enough to know the answer – no!

This process is hugely cumbersome. It'll only invite trouble and pain. You need a system which is smart and intelligent enough to auto load your files and extract dependencies. The answer is 'Composer'.

Let me explain why and how this "Composer" makes your life much easier.

Suppose you name your application – PHP7BOOK. You'd like to use that namespace all through your application. Very nice. First you create a JSON file – composer.json – inside your application main folder.

```
1   //composer.json
2   {
3       "autoload": {
4           "psr-4": {
5               "PHP7BOOK\\": "source"
6           }
7       }
8   }
```

You may ask, what is "psr-4"? For now consider it as a standard that'll auto load files. The convention is you point your 'source' directory to the name of the application – PHP7BOOK.

Once you've done that, the files inside the 'source' folder are in the global namespace. Now you can use 'PHP7BOOK' on top of any file and pull any file staying at that namespace.

What's more, any developer now can add any file to the source folder and just update 'composer'. It's done. Another developer sitting in a distant part of the globe can pull in that file and work on it.

The first step is opening your terminal and issuing this command:

```
1   composer install
```

It'll install a 'vendor' file inside the root directory of your 'PHP7BOOK' application.

The output on your terminal looks like this:

```
1   Loading composer repositories with package information
2   Updating dependencies (including require-dev)
3   Nothing to install or update
4   Generating autoload files
```

Now inside your application there is a 'vendor' folder which must have a folder 'composer' and a file called 'autoload.php'. The file reads like this:

```
1   <?php
2
3   // autoload.php @generated by Composer
4   require_once __DIR__ . '/composer' . '/autoload_real.php';
5
6   return ComposerAutoloaderInit28544d5df40d4cd20ca5c80089b74c19::getLoader();
```

And now comes the best part.

Issue another command on your terminal.

```
1   composer dump-autoload
```

And inside your 'vendor/composer' folder you'll find a file 'autoload_psr4.php'.

This file actually holds the key of pointing your namespace 'PHP7BOOK' to the 'source' folder. It reads like this:

```
1   <?php
2
3   // autoload_psr4.php @generated by Composer
4
5   $vendorDir = dirname(dirname(__FILE__));
6   $baseDir = dirname($vendorDir);
7
8   return array(
9       'PHP7BOOK\\' => array($baseDir . '/source'),
10  );
11
12  Look at the last line:
13
14  'PHP7BOOK\\' => array($baseDir . '/source'),
```

It indicates exactly what you've wanted. Now you can use 'PHP7BOOK' namespace and it'll rightly point to the 'source' folder.

In the 'source' folder we have three files: Word, Dictionary and Meaning.

```
1   //source/Word.php
2   <?php
3   namespace PHP7BOOK;
4   class Word {
5
6       protected $words;
7
8       public function __construct($words) {
9           $this->words = $words;
10      }
11  }
```

Next comes Dictionary file.

```
1   //source/Dictionary.php
2   <?php
3   use PHP7BOOK\Meaning;
4   use PHP7BOOK\Dictionary;
5   use PHP7BOOK\Word;
6
7   $meaning = new Meaning();
8   $marrion = new Dictionary($meaning);
9   $firstWord = new Word("The Noun 'a' has seven senses.");
10  $marrion->setMeaning($firstWord);
11  $secondWord = new Word("The noun 'aa' has three senses.");
12  $marrion->setMeaning($secondWord);
13
14  var_dump($marrion->getMeaning());
```

And finally comes the file 'Meaning.php'.

```
1   //source/Meaning.php
2   <?php
3   namespace PHP7BOOK;
4   class Meaning {
5
6       protected $definitions = [];
7
8       public function setWords(Word $words) {
9           $this->definitions[] = $words;
10      }
11
12      public function getWords() {
13          return $this->definitions;
14      }
15  }
```

Our application is almost ready. We need a 'dictionary.php' file where we can instantiate our objects.

```php
1   //dictionary.php
2   <?php
3   use PHP7BOOK\Meaning;
4   use PHP7BOOK\Dictionary;
5   use PHP7BOOK\Word;
6
7
8   $meaning = new Meaning();
9
10  $marrion = new Dictionary($meaning);
11
12  $firstWord = new Word("The Noun 'a' has seven senses.");
13  $marrion->setMeaning($firstWord);
14  $secondWord = new Word("The noun 'aa' has three senses.");
15  $marrion->setMeaning($secondWord);
16
17  var_dump($marrion->getMeaning());
```

Finally you should assure that each time you run the application every files be auto loaded. For that reason you can either create an index file or name it simply as 'entry.php'.

Only two lines of code suffice.

```php
1   //entry.php
2   <?php
3
4   require 'vendor/autoload.php';
5   require 'dictionary.php';
```

Now your dictionary application is ready run. Not only that, all through this creating process you have maintained the SOLID design principle. Your objects are loosely coupled and they move and pass on messages among them independently.

Factory Patterns and Singleton Patterns

As you've already known that there are numerous ways to structure your code. It depends on your project. It depends on the size or magnitude of the project. You can put as little or as much effort as you wish in planning.

Factory pattern is one of them. And probably it's the most commonly used pattern. In factory pattern you just simply use a class to create an object out of it.

Consider this example.

```php
1   <?php
2
3   class WebService {
4
5       private $hostingService;
6       private $designService;
7
8       public function __construct($hostingService, $designService) {
9           $this->hostingService = $hostingService;
10          $this->designService = $designService;
11      }
12
13      public function HostingAndDesigning() {
14          return $this->hostingService . " " . $this->designService;
15      }
16  }
17
18  class WebFactory {
19      public static function getHostingAndDesigning(int $hostingService, int $desi\
20  gnService) {
21          return new WebService($hostingService, $designService);
22      }
23  }
24
25  $client = WebFactory::getHostingAndDesigning(250, 1200);
26  //var_dump($client->HostingAndDesigning());
27  print_r($client->HostingAndDesigning());
```

And here is the output.

```
1   250 1200
```

Here your code creates 'Web Factory' to get hosting and designing services. You may ask what the benefit is.

The major benefit is later you can change, rename or replace the 'WebService' class. In that case you'll only have to change in the factory. The second benefit is you can manage the amount in your factory. You need not create new instance for each client.

Consider the last part of your previous code. We just have another client who wants to services and you order your factory to get her web services.

```
1   $client = WebFactory::getHostingAndDesigning(250, 1200);
2   print_r($client->HostingAndDesigning());
3   $client1 = WebFactory::getHostingAndDesigning(320, 1500);
4   print_r($client1->HostingAndDesigning());
```

Look at the output now.

```
1   250 1200
2   320 1500
```

Any design pattern is actually the repeatable solution to the problems that commonly occur.

The better part is that you can design your factory pattern in numerous ways. Let us imagine a hosting factory where we're supposed to give two types of services – general hosting and dedicated hosting. In the factory class we'll set the id and name of the clients.

Incidentally our first two clients have similar names – "Sanjib". And both want general hosting.

How you can tackle this problem?

First of all you can set a hosting factory class. It could be abstract. Or you might have used an interface instead of an abstract class. You chose the abstract method.

In that case, the code snippet may look like this.

```php
1   <?php
2
3
4
5   abstract class HostingService {
6
7       private $id;
8       private $name;
9       protected $type = null;
10
11      public function __construct(int $id, $name) {
12        $this->id = $id;
13        $this->name = $name;
14      }
15
16      public function getID() {
17          return $this->id;
18      }
19
20      public function getName() {
21          return $this->name;
22      }
23
24      public function getType() {
25          return $this->type;
26      }
27  }
28
29
30
31  class GeneralPlan extends HostingService {
32      protected $type = "General";
33  }
34
35  class DedicatedPlan extends HostingService {
36      protected $type = "Dedicated";
37  }
38
39  $clientSanjib_001 = new GeneralPlan(1, "Sanjib_001");
40  var_dump($clientSanjib_001);
41  $clientSanjib_002 = new GeneralPlan(2, "Sanjib_002");
42  var_dump($clientSanjib_002);
```

Let us see the output first.

```
1   object(GeneralPlan)#1 (3) {
2     ["type":protected]=>
3     string(7) "General"
4     ["id":"HostingService":private]=>
5     int(1)
6     ["name":"HostingService":private]=>
7     string(10) "Sanjib_001"
8   }
9   object(GeneralPlan)#2 (3) {
10    ["type":protected]=>
11    string(7) "General"
12    ["id":"HostingService":private]=>
13    int(2)
14    ["name":"HostingService":private]=>
15    string(10) "Sanjib_002"
16  }
```

For the first client – Sanjib – we have everything covered. Type, id and name. For distinction we name them as "Sanjib_001" and "Sanjib_002".

It was not necessary. We could have named them as "Sanjib" only because we have different IDs. Now you have been asked to add another client. Suppose her name is "SomeoneElse".

Now it's become extremely easy. Add two lines at the end of your code snippet.

```
1   $clientSomeElse = new GeneralPlan(3, "SomeoneElse");
2   var_dump($clientSomeElse);
```

Now here is your new output.

```
1   object(GeneralPlan)#1 (3) {
2     ["type":protected]=>
3     string(7) "General"
4     ["id":"HostingService":private]=>
5     int(1)
6     ["name":"HostingService":private]=>
7     string(10) "Sanjib_001"
8   }
9   object(GeneralPlan)#2 (3) {
10    ["type":protected]=>
11    string(7) "General"
```

```
12    ["id":"HostingService":private]=>
13    int(2)
14    ["name":"HostingService":private]=>
15    string(10) "Sanjib_002"
16  }
17  object(GeneralPlan)#3 (3) {
18    ["type":protected]=>
19    string(7) "General"
20    ["id":"HostingService":private]=>
21    int(3)
22    ["name":"HostingService":private]=>
23    string(11) "SomeoneElse"
24  }
```

All along we've kept our ID and name private and only the type is protected. Well done! You have encapsulated your logic for instantiating and furthermore you've reduced the tight coupling of the objects.

Now we have another client who wants dedicated service, not the general one. And incidentally the client's name is "SomeoneElse". It sounds very funny to have clients having similar names. But the real fun is we're not at all worried.

Why?

Because we have a factory class and it's been well defined to tackle this type of funny problems.

We are not going to add any number any more with new client "SomeoneElse". We'd just like to add him with the id 1. Remember this is our first client in the dedicated service type or category. And we've defined that in our abstract factory. So without worrying at all we just add the new client at the end of our previous code snippet.

```
1   $clientSomeElse = new DedicatedPlan(1, "SomeoneElse");
2   var_dump($clientSomeElse);
```

And look at the final output now.

```
1   object(GeneralPlan)#1 (3) {
2     ["type":protected]=>
3     string(7) "General"
4     ["id":"HostingService":private]=>
5     int(1)
6     ["name":"HostingService":private]=>
7     string(10) "Sanjib_001"
8   }
9   object(GeneralPlan)#2 (3) {
10    ["type":protected]=>
11    string(7) "General"
12    ["id":"HostingService":private]=>
13    int(2)
14    ["name":"HostingService":private]=>
15    string(10) "Sanjib_002"
16  }
17  object(GeneralPlan)#3 (3) {
18    ["type":protected]=>
19    string(7) "General"
20    ["id":"HostingService":private]=>
21    int(3)
22    ["name":"HostingService":private]=>
23    string(11) "SomeoneElse"
24  }
25  object(DedicatedPlan)#4 (3) {
26    ["type":protected]=>
27    string(9) "Dedicated"
28    ["id":"HostingService":private]=>
29    int(1)
30    ["name":"HostingService":private]=>
31    string(11) "SomeoneElse"
32  }
```

Now you could maintain thousands of different clients without worrying about the application classes. They know the object types at the run time. They cannot anticipate it beforehand.

Day 4

We've traversed almost half of the whole journey and at present we are in the middle of learning design patterns.

The fourth day will start with decorator patterns. Then we'll learn about chain of responsibility – a popular design pattern.

Finally we'll know about more architecture.

Decorating Applications

When we want to add additional features to our existing classes we generally use decorator pattern.

Do you find this definition useful?

I believe the answer will be NO.

It says about only adding new features. It doesn't say about how you will use that. Will you add the features by simply hard coding or you'll add them in the run time.

That's a pretty big difference.

Why?

Let us consider a simple example where we are talking about a hosting company. A typical hosting company sells hosting services and sometimes they also provide template designing.

Let's design a pretty basic scenario.

```php
1   <?php
2
3   // a Web service center
4
5   class HostingService {
6
7       public function Cost() {
8
9           return 20;
10      }
11  }
12
13  class TemplateDesign {
14
15      protected $hosting = 10;
16
17      public function Desisn() {
18          return $this->hosting + 15;
19      }
20  }
21
22  $CostofHosting = new HostingService();
23  //var_dump($CostofHosting->Cost());
```

```
24   $HostingAndDesign = new TemplateDesign();
25   var_dump($HostingAndDesign->Desisn());
```

It's a very basic hosting application where if you want to get only hosting services it will cost 20 dollar. If you want to go for the both – hosting and template designing – then there is a discount. In such cases, the hosting services will be half.

Where is the flaw in this code?

It runs fine. When we run it for only hosting service it returns 20. And when we run it for hosting and designing, it returns 25.

The real problem lies in adding new features. When the template design part has been added with hosting services, we have to hard code the discount. Imagine a situation where you have decided to increase hosting cost. You need to hard code that cost into your hosting class first. Next you need to calculate and make the amount half in the combined hosting and design class.

This is a real problem. It cannot go on this way. But you need to add features. How you can overcome this problem?

The decorator pattern is the answer where you can design your application in such a way that will allow you to add features in the run time.

Moreover, when you work in a group, your friends can also participate. Consider this code snippet first.

```php
1    <?php
2
3    // a Web service center
4
5    interface WebService {
6        public function getDescription();
7        public function getCost();
8    }
9
10   class HostingService implements WebService {
11
12       public function getDescription() {
13           return "Hosting services cost ";
14       }
15       public function getCost() {
16
17           return 2000;
18       }
19   }
20
```

```
21   class WebDesign implements WebService {
22
23       protected $websrvice;
24
25       public function __construct(WebService $webservice) {
26           $this->websrvice = $webservice;
27       }
28
29       public function getDescription() {
30           return "The web designing costs ";
31       }
32
33       public function getCost() {
34           return 1500 . "\n";
35       }
36
37       public function HostingAndDesigning() {
38           return 1500 + $this->websrvice->getCost() - $this->websrvice->getCost() \
39   * 20 / 100 . " . For "
40                     . "hosting and designing jointly you"
41                     . " save " . $this->websrvice->getCost() * 20 / 100 . "\n";          \
42
43       }
44   }
45   $CostofHosting = new HostingService();
46   $webdesign = new WebDesign($CostofHosting);
47   echo $webdesign->getDescription();
48   echo $webdesign->getCost();
49   echo $webdesign->getDescription() . " with hosting ";
50   echo $webdesign->HostingAndDesigning();
```

We have decided to use a contract first. What is contract? That will keep things hidden from the original classes. It will encapsulate our application.

Watch the first part of the code.

```
1    interface WebService {
2        public function getDescription();
3        public function getCost();
4    }
```

We want description and the cost of the web services that you're going to provide. For brevity we imagine your web services company provide hosting services and web design services. Let us first think about the hosting services.

```
1   class HostingService implements WebService {
2
3       public function getDescription() {
4           return "Hosting services cost ";
5       }
6       public function getCost() {
7
8           return 2000;
9       }
10  }
```

Very simple. Along with the description it also shows the cost – that returns 2000 dollar. (If you think it's too much, please bear with it. It's just an example.)

The third part is important where you're supposed to add new features. For this case you have added web design services along with the hosting services. We'll have getDescription() and getCost() methods. But you have also decided to inject another service into it - HostingAndDesigning(). If someone wants to buy both features – hosting and designing – she'll get a 20 percent discount on the hosting services.

```
1   class WebDesign implements WebService {
2
3       protected $websrvice;
4
5       public function __construct(WebService $webservice) {
6           $this->websrvice = $webservice;
7       }
8
9       public function getDescription() {
10          return "The web designing costs ";
11      }
12
13      public function getCost() {
14          return 1500 . "\n";
15      }
16
17      public function HostingAndDesigning() {
18          return 1500 + $this->websrvice->getCost() - $this->websrvice->getCost() \
19  * 20 / 100 . " . For "
20                        . "hosting and designing jointly you"
21                        . " save " . $this->websrvice->getCost() * 20 / 100 . "\n";        \
22
23      }
24  }
```

Run the code, you'll see this output:

```
1  Hosting services cost 2000
2  The web designing costs 1500
3  The web designing costs with hosting 3100. For hosting and designing jointly you\
4    save 400
```

You have used decorator pattern and added new features. Now suddenly you decide to change the hosting services cost and want to make it 200 instead of 2000. If such situation arises, you needn't have to worry about hard coding the code in every class. Just change it in you're your second part of the code:

```
1  class HostingService implements WebService {
2
3      public function getDescription() {
4          return "Hosting services cost ";
5      }
6      public function getCost() {
7
8          return 200 . "\n";
9      }
10 }
```

Now see the magic in your output.

```
1  Hosting services cost 200
2  The web designing costs 1500
3  The web designing costs with hosting 1660. For hosting and designing jointly you\
4    save 40
```

Everything changes in the run time due to using the decorator pattern. Even more importantly you can keep adding on new features in your application.

Are you ready to get started in adding new features? Shall we begin? Let us imagine a situation where web designing services will be modified with few other services like wordpress designing and drupal designing. You are ready to give your client special web designing services where more options are available.

Now you can use abstract class. This abstract class will indicate that your application is segmented just in the web designing section. It doesn't touch the hosting services segment. This abstract class is handling with the web design part only. Now the full code looks like this.

```php
1   <?php
2
3   // a Web service center
4
5   interface WebService {
6       public function getDescription();
7       public function getCost();
8   }
9
10  class HostingService implements WebService {
11
12      public function getDescription() {
13          return "Hosting services cost ";
14      }
15      public function getCost() {
16
17          return 200 . "\n";
18      }
19  }
20
21  class WebDesign implements WebService {
22
23      protected $websrvice;
24
25      public function __construct(WebService $webservice) {
26          $this->websrvice = $webservice;
27      }
28
29      public function getDescription() {
30          return "The web designing costs ";
31      }
32
33      public function getCost() {
34          return 1500 . "\n";
35      }
36
37      public function HostingAndDesigning() {
38          return 1500 + $this->websrvice->getCost() - $this->websrvice->getCost() \
39  * 20 / 100 . " . For "
40                  . "hosting and designing jointly you"
41                  . " save " . $this->websrvice->getCost() * 20 / 100 . "\n";      \
42
```

```
43        }
44    }
45
46    abstract class WebDesignFeatures implements WebService {
47        protected $webdesign;
48        public function __construct(WebDesign $webdesign) {
49            $this->webdesign = $webdesign;
50        }
51        public function getDescription(){
52            $this->webdesign->getDescription();
53        }
54        public function getCost() {
55            $this->webdesign->getCost();
56        }
57    }
58
59
60    class WordpressDesign extends WebDesignFeatures {
61
62        protected $webdesign;
63
64        public function getDescription() {
65            return $this->webdesign->getDescription() . " with wordpress designing: \
66    ";
67        }
68
69        public function getCost() {
70            return $this->webdesign->getCost() + 2000 . "\n";
71        }
72    }
73
74    class DrupalDesign extends WebDesignFeatures {
75
76        protected $webdesign;
77
78        public function getDescription() {
79            return $this->webdesign->getDescription() . " with drupal designing: ";
80        }
81
82        public function getCost() {
83            return $this->webdesign->getCost() + 2500 . "\n";
84        }
```

```
85  }
86
87  $CostofHosting = new HostingService();
88  echo $CostofHosting->getDescription();
89  echo $CostofHosting->getCost();
90  $webdesign = new WebDesign($CostofHosting);
91  echo $webdesign->getDescription();
92  echo $webdesign->getCost();
93  echo $webdesign->getDescription() . " with hosting ";
94  echo $webdesign->HostingAndDesigning();
95
96  $wordpressdesign = new WebDesign($CostofHosting);
97  $templateandwordpress = new WordpressDesign($wordpressdesign);
98  echo $templateandwordpress->getDescription();
99  echo $templateandwordpress->getCost();
100
101 $drupaldesign = new WebDesign($CostofHosting);
102 $templateanddrupal = new DrupalDesign($drupaldesign);
103 echo $templateanddrupal->getDescription();
104 echo $templateanddrupal->getCost();
```

Let us see what our output says.

```
1  Hosting services cost 200
2  The web designing costs 1500
3  The web designing costs with hosting 1660. For hosting and designing jointly you\
4   save 40
5  The web designing costs with wordpress designing: 3500
6  The web designing costs with drupal designing: 4000
```

Now if you want you can add any feature anywhere. You can change any part and you don't have to hard code it into your application. Suppose you want to add a discount only in the wordpress designing segment. The other part of the application is not affected.

Our application follows the SOLID design principle and objects are loosely coupled.

Responsibility Unchained

In object-oriented design, the chain-of-responsibility pattern belongs to behavioral design patterns segment. The simplest example contains a person using ATM. He's entering pin, receiving payment and receipts etcetera.

What is behavioral design pattern? They are a type of design patterns that generally identify communicating objects.

You may ask, what kind of objects we're talking about? These objects have common communication patterns between them. While communicating they must realize that patterns.

In a glance it seems that the definition is a bit fuzzy. When I started with 'chain of responsibility pattern', I've found it rather unclear. But thing is, once you understand the basic concepts, you'd love its potential qualities.

In this pattern one object communicates with the other and in doing so, these patterns increase flexibility in carrying out this communication.

This pattern consists of source of command objects and a series of processing objects. So we need a 'processor' and the 'next' command that actually delegates its responsibility to the other object and each processing object contains a certain type of logic that describes the types of command objects that it can handle.

It processes a part and then the rest are passed to the next processing object in the chain. Let us assume a calculator. It adds, subtracts, multiplies and divides. Each object does its job and passes the processing job to the next one.

Consider this code.

```php
<?php

abstract class Calculate {

    protected $successor;

    public function check(Calculator $calculate){

    }

    public function calculateWith(Calculate $successor) {
        $this->successor = $successor;
    }
```

```
14
15     public function next(Calculator $calculate) {
16         if ($this->successor){
17             $this->successor->check($calculate);
18         }
19     }
20  }
21
22  class Adds extends Calculate {
23
24     public function check(Calculator $calculate) {
25
26         if (!$calculate->add){
27
28             throw new Exception("Addition has not been done! Please check.");
29
30         }
31
32         $this->next($calculate);
33     }
34
35  }
36
37  class Subtracts extends Calculate {
38
39     public function check(Calculator $calculate) {
40
41         if (!$calculate->sub){
42
43             throw new Exception("Subtraction has not been done! Please check.");
44
45         }
46
47         $this->next($calculate);
48     }
49
50  }
51
52  class Mulitiply extends Calculate {
53
54     public function check(Calculator $calculate) {
55
```

```
56          if (!$calculate->mul){
57
58              throw new Exception("Multiplicatiotion has not been done! Please che\
59   ck.");
60
61          }
62
63          $this->next($calculate);
64      }
65
66   }
67
68   class Divide extends Calculate {
69
70       public function check(Calculator $calculate) {
71
72          if (!$calculate->div){
73
74              throw new Exception("Division has not been done! Please check.");
75
76          }
77
78          $this->next($calculate);
79      }
80
81   }
82
83   class Calculator {
84
85       public $add = true;
86       public $sub = true;
87       public $mul = true;
88       public $div = true;
89   }
90
91   $add = new Adds();
92
93   $sub = new Subtracts();
94
95   $mul = new Mulitiply();
96
97   $div = new Divide();
```

```
98
99   $add->calculateWith($sub);
100  $sub->calculateWith($mul);
101  $mul->calculateWith($div);
102
103  $add->check(new Calculator());
```

The first part of the code is the "Calculator" class which defines each property to be true. We assume a situation where addition, subtraction, multiplication and division properties are true. When they are true, the application would not throw any error message. But when one comes out as false, it'll first checks which one is false and throw error message accordingly. The first client object that performs the request and sets up the chain is 'add'.

Look at the part of the code section.

```
1    $add = new Adds();
2
3    $sub = new Subtracts();
4
5    $mul = new Mulitiply();
6
7    $div = new Divide();
8
9    $add->calculateWith($sub);
10   $sub->calculateWith($mul);
11   $mul->calculateWith($div);
```

Here '$add' object sets up the chain. If the property of '$add' is false, error will be thrown. The chain is affected immediately.

In the middle part if '$mul' or multiplication object comes out as false, the chain is affected in the middle.

We'll see each output. In the beginning, we assume that the addition property is not true. Let us see what we get in our output.

```
1  PHP Fatal error:  Uncaught Exception: Addition has not been done! Please check. \
2  in /home/hagudu/Code/php7book1/Day4/chain1.php:28
3  Stack trace:
4  #0 /home/hagudu/Code/php7book1/Day4/chain1.php(102): Adds->check(Object(Calculat\
5  or))
6  #1 {main}
7    thrown in /home/hagudu/Code/php7book1/Day4/chain1.php on line 28
```

The very first line of the chain has been affected; so it does not proceed any more.

Let us make the subtraction property false and see the output.

```
1  PHP Fatal error:  Uncaught Exception: Subtraction has not been done! Please chec\
2  k. in /home/hagudu/Code/php7book1/Day4/chain1.php:43
3  Stack trace:
4  #0 /home/hagudu/Code/php7book1/Day4/chain1.php(17): Subtracts->check(Object(Calc\
5  ulator))
6  #1 /home/hagudu/Code/php7book1/Day4/chain1.php(32): Calculate->next(Object(Calcu\
7  lator))
8  #2 /home/hagudu/Code/php7book1/Day4/chain1.php(102): Adds->check(Object(Calculat\
9  or))
10 #3 {main}
11   thrown in /home/hagudu/Code/php7book1/Day4/chain1.php on line 43
```

Next we'll make the multiplication property false and see the output.

```
1  PHP Fatal error:  Uncaught Exception: Multiplicatiotion has not been done! Pleas\
2  e check. in /home/hagudu/Code/php7book1/Day4/chain1.php:58
3  Stack trace:
4  #0 /home/hagudu/Code/php7book1/Day4/chain1.php(17): Mulitiply->check(Object(Calc\
5  ulator))
6  #1 /home/hagudu/Code/php7book1/Day4/chain1.php(47): Calculate->next(Object(Calcu\
7  lator))
8  #2 /home/hagudu/Code/php7book1/Day4/chain1.php(17): Subtracts->check(Object(Calc\
9  ulator))
10 #3 /home/hagudu/Code/php7book1/Day4/chain1.php(32): Calculate->next(Object(Calcu\
11 lator))
12 #4 /home/hagudu/Code/php7book1/Day4/chain1.php(102): Adds->check(Object(Calculat\
13 or))
14 #5 {main}
15   thrown in /home/hagudu/Code/php7book1/Day4/chain1.php on line 58
```

You have probably noticed that the lines of output have been increased as we move towards the lower segment of the chain.

Inspect the stack trace. It starts with multiply checking. Then it hits the 'next' button and proceeds to check the previous object.

```
1   #0 /home/hagudu/Code/php7book1/Day4/chain1.php(17): Mulitiply->check(Object(Calc\
2   ulator))
3   #1 /home/hagudu/Code/php7book1/Day4/chain1.php(47): Calculate->next(Object(Calcu\
4   lator))
```

Lastly we'll make the division property false and see the output.

```
1    PHP Fatal error:  Uncaught Exception: Division has not been done! Please check.\
2    in /home/hagudu/Code/php7book1/Day4/chain1.php:73
3    Stack trace:
4    #0 /home/hagudu/Code/php7book1/Day4/chain1.php(17): Divide->check(Object(Calcula\
5    tor))
6    #1 /home/hagudu/Code/php7book1/Day4/chain1.php(62): Calculate->next(Object(Calcu\
7    lator))
8    #2 /home/hagudu/Code/php7book1/Day4/chain1.php(17): Mulitiply->check(Object(Calc\
9    ulator))
10   #3 /home/hagudu/Code/php7book1/Day4/chain1.php(47): Calculate->next(Object(Calcu\
11   lator))
12   #4 /home/hagudu/Code/php7book1/Day4/chain1.php(17): Subtracts->check(Object(Calc\
13   ulator))
14   #5 /home/hagudu/Code/php7book1/Day4/chain1.php(32): Calculate->next(Object(Calcu\
15   lator))
16   #6 /home/hagudu/Code/php7book1/Day4/chain1.php(102): Adds->check(Object(Calculat\
17   or))
18   #7 {main}
19     thrown in /home/hagudu/Code/php7book1/Day4/chain1.php on line 73
```

Two more lines have been added to the stack trace.

This chain of responsibility pattern includes a handler. It could be either an interface or an abstract class. In our case we have made it an abstract class. It sets the successor in the chain. And the total operation has been done by a series of processing jobs. All the handlers are the part of the chain.

Adapt SMS into MAIL

Now we're going to do an impossible task.

Are you prepared?

Can we start?

This chapter is about the adapter pattern. It's one of the design patterns that you're currently on. Let us start with a real world example.

You know that internet connection is absolutely necessary for sending emails. Is it true in the real world? You'd say, well, I know that. An internet networking is a must.

Can we solve this problem by using some intermediary method? Situation may come where you go to a place where internet connection is not available at all. Or it's very weak indeed to send an important mail.

What's to be done in that situation?

There is a solution.

Adapter!

Yes, there we can choose IFTTT as the adapter. IFTTT is a service that supports automating tasks with popular API's. Thus we can use IFTTT as the adapter to convert our SMS to MAIL.

What's happening behind the scene is: IFTTT service communicates with the internet and just changes your SMS into MAIL. In a land with no internet connection cannot restrict you sending mails any more!

In essence this is all about adapter patterns in PHP.

An adapter, basically, helps two incompatible interfaces to work mutually. It sounds nice but the task is not so pleasant. The interfaces we're talking about may seem to be incompatible but their inner functionality should match and work at tandem.

Imagine a situation where the client expects an interface but at that moment you cannot supply that. You have a completely different interface. So you use an adapter and that adapter translates your interface into the client's interface. So the client shouldn't change her interface but actually gets a completely different interface through that adapter.

Your client expects a mail but at present you don't have any internet connection. You have a mobile and you can send a SMS. But your SMS should have been translated into a MAIL by the time when it reaches the client.

You use IFTTT adapter and that service converts your SMS to MAIL.

Let us see how we can do that in our code.

First, you think about a simple 'Mobile' class that sends SMS and a "Person" class receives that SMS.

```php
1   <?php
2
3
4   class Mobile {
5
6       public function sendMessage() {
7
8           var_dump("You have a new SMS.");
9
10      }
11
12  }
13
14  class Person {
15
16      public function recieve($message) {
17          $message->sendMessage();
18      }
19  }
20
21  $person = new Person();
22  echo $person->recieve(new Mobile());
```

The output is obvious. Now we can use an interface for lose coupling of our class object so that we can develop this code into this.

```php
1   <?php
2
3   interface MobileInterface {
4       public function sendMessage();
5   }
6
7
8   class Mobile implements MobileInterface {
9
10      public function sendMessage() {
11
12          var_dump("You have a new SMS.");
13
14      }
```

```
15
16  }
17
18  class Person {
19
20      public function recieve(MobileInterface $message) {
21          $message->sendMessage();
22      }
23  }
24
25  $person = new Person();
26  echo $person->recieve(new Mobile());
```

The output remains same. It's not changed. Now we'd like to have a 'Mail' class where we can send a mail. We've done the same thing through our 'Mobile' class. We also use another Mail interface for making our code loosely coupled. We also try an impossible task. We want that the person should get a mail through the mobile interface. Watch the last line carefully.

```
1   <?php
2
3   interface MobileInterface {
4       public function sendMessage();
5   }
6
7   interface MailInterface {
8       public function sendMail();
9   }
10
11
12  class Mobile implements MobileInterface {
13
14      public function sendMessage() {
15
16          var_dump("You have a new SMS.");
17
18      }
19
20  }
21
22  class Mail implements MailInterface {
23
24      public function sendMail() {
```

```
25
26            var_dump("You have a new MAIL.");
27
28        }
29
30  }
31
32
33  class Person {
34
35      public function recieve(MobileInterface $message) {
36          $message->sendMessage();
37      }
38  }
39
40  $person = new Person();
41  echo $person->recieve(new Mail());
```

What will be the output?

What you're expecting is correct. It'll give an error.

```
1  PHP Fatal error:  Uncaught TypeError: Argument 1 passed to Person::recieve() mus\
2  t implement interface MobileInterface, instance of Mail given, called in /home/h\
3  agudu/Code/php7book1/Day4/adapter.php on line 41 and defined in /home/hagudu/Cod\
4  e/php7book1/Day4/adapter.php:35
5  Stack trace:
6  #0 /home/hagudu/Code/php7book1/Day4/adapter.php(41): Person->recieve(Object(Mail\
7  ))
8  #1 {main}
9    thrown in /home/hagudu/Code/php7book1/Day4/adapter.php on line 35
```

You have no internet connection but you want that your SMS will be converted to MAIL and the person will receive that. It's impossible.

You can make it possible only if you can use an adapter. An adapter, that'll convert your SMS into MAIL.

To do that we write an adapter class that actually uses mobile interface to send SMS. And while doing that it will use 'Mail' class in its constructor so that mail object can convert your SMS into MAIL.

Watch the adapter class carefully.

```
1   class IFTTTadapter implements MobileInterface {
2
3       private $ifttt;
4
5       public function __construct(Mail $message) {
6           $this->ifttt = $message;
7       }
8
9       public function sendMessage() {
10          $this->ifttt->sendMail();
11      }
12  }
```

When the 'IFTTTadapter' class is in place, you can safely send SMS like this:

```
1   class Person {
2
3       public function recieve(MobileInterface $message) {
4           $message->sendMessage();
5       }
6   }
7
8   $person = new Person();
9   echo $person->recieve(new Mobile());
```

And it'll give you an output like this:

```
1   string(8) "You have a new SMS."
```

But what happens when you use the IFTTTadapter? The whole bunch of code looks like this:

```
1   <?php
2
3   interface MobileInterface {
4       public function sendMessage();
5   }
6
7   interface MailInterface {
8       public function sendMail();
9   }
10
```

```
11   class IFTTTadapter implements MobileInterface {
12
13       private $ifttt;
14
15       public function __construct(Mail $message) {
16           $this->ifttt = $message;
17       }
18
19       public function sendMessage() {
20           $this->ifttt->sendMail();
21       }
22   }
23
24
25   class Mobile implements MobileInterface {
26
27       public function sendMessage() {
28
29           var_dump("You have a new SMS.");
30
31       }
32
33   }
34
35   class Mail implements MailInterface {
36
37       public function sendMail() {
38
39           var_dump("You have a new MAIL.");
40
41       }
42
43   }
44
45
46   class Person {
47
48       public function recieve(MobileInterface $message) {
49           $message->sendMessage();
50       }
51   }
52
```

```
53  $person = new Person();
54  echo $person->recieve(new IFTTTadapter(new Mail()));
```

The last part of the code is extremely important.

```
1  class Person {
2
3      public function recieve(MobileInterface $message) {
4          $message->sendMessage();
5      }
6  }
7
8  $person = new Person();
9  echo $person->recieve(new IFTTTadapter(new Mail()));
```

The person or client class remains unchanged. It sends message through 'Mobile Interface'. And finally the person object or client receives it through IFTTTadapter class and Mail method. So the output comes out as expected.

```
1  string(8) "You have a new MAIL."
```

Finally we can conclude that adapter pattern works as a connection between two incompatible interfaces. It belongs to structural design pattern as this pattern converts one independent interface to act as another without inviting any trouble.

Day 5

We'll start with the Template Pattern and then we'll learn about the relationships between classes which are extremely important when you design a big project.

Finally we'll explore the useful static variables and static functions.

We'll also see ehether the singleton pattern can come to any help in such cases.

The Template Pattern

Template pattern is used prominently in php frameworks where an abstract class uses one similar method that sub classes share between them.

Imagine a situation where men and machines perform almost same tasks. In such cases we can separate them into different classes or we can associate them through a center class or template class. So a template is there and the sub classes will follow that template since they have a lot of similarities in their actions.

Let us consider two separate classes "Man" and "machine".

First, we think about the "Man" class.

```
1  class Man {
2
3      public function work() {
4
5          $this->getUp()->goToWork()->manWork()->returnToBase()->sleep();
6
7      }
8
9      public function getUp() {
10         var_dump("Get up man, you need to go to work now.");
11         return $this;
12     }
13
14     public function goToWork() {
15         var_dump("We're going to work now.");
16         return $this;
17     }
18
19     public function manWork() {
20         var_dump("Supervising the machines and instruct them to work.");
21         return $this;
22     }
23
24     public function returnToBase() {
25         var_dump("Now it's time to return to home and spend time with family.");
26         return $this;
27     }
```

```
28
29    public function sleep() {
30        var_dump("Get rest so you can work tomorrow again.");
31        return $this;
32    }
33 }
34 $worker = new Man();
35 $worker->work();
```

The output is quite obvious.

```
1  string(39) "Get up man, you need to go to work now."
2  string(24) "We're going to work now."
3  string(51) "Supervising the machines and instruct them to work."
4  string(59) "Now it's time to return to home and spend time with family."
5  string(40) "Get rest so you can work tomorrow again."
```

Now we'll think about the "Machine" class.

```
1  class Machine {
2
3      public function work() {
4
5          $this->getUp()->goToWork()->machineWork()->returnToBase()->sleep();
6
7      }
8
9      public function getUp() {
10         var_dump("Get up man, you need to go to work now.");
11         return $this;
12     }
13
14     public function goToWork() {
15         var_dump("We're going to work now.");
16         return $this;
17     }
18
19     public function machineWork() {
20         var_dump("Take instruction and work accordingly.");
21         return $this;
22     }
23
```

```
24      public function returnToBase() {
25          var_dump("Now it's time to return to home and spend time with family.");
26          return $this;
27      }
28
29      public function sleep() {
30          var_dump("Get rest so you can work tomorrow again.");
31          return $this;
32      }
33  }
34  $worker = new Machine();
35  $worker->work();
```

The output will be like before with a slight change in the behavior of the new worker.

```
1   string(39) "Get up man, you need to go to work now."
2   string(24) "We're going to work now."
3   string(38) "Take instruction and work accordingly."
4   string(59) "Now it's time to return to home and spend time with family."
5   string(40) "Get rest so you can work tomorrow again."
```

In "Man" class we have defined a method:

```
1   public function manWork() {
2           var_dump("Supervising the machines and instruct them to work.");
3           return $this;
4       }
```

And in "Machine" class we've defined the same method in a different name:

```
1   public function machineWork() {
2           var_dump("Take instruction and work accordingly.");
3           return $this;
4       }
```

When a man or woman works, he or she gives instructions to the machines. But when a machine works, it takes instructions from machine operators and work accordingly.

These types of classes are perfect candidates for template patterns.

Why?

It's because, they both have similar methods of actions. They get up, go to work, work, come back and take rest.

The only difference has been the way of working. A man gives instructions and the machine listens to that instructions and perform accordingly. The major parts of their actions follow the same route. We can define them in an abstract class. The point of difference can also be solved by an abstract method. It can be the template and the sub classes can either blindly follow them or they can override them according to their wishes.

The final template pattern may look like this:

```php
<?php

abstract class ManMachine {

    public function work() {

        $this->getUp()->goToWork()->commonWork()->returnToBase()->sleep();

    }

    protected function getUp() {
        var_dump("Get up man, you need to go to work now.");
        return $this;
    }

    protected function goToWork() {
        var_dump("We're going to work now.");
        return $this;
    }

    protected abstract function commonWork();

    protected function returnToBase() {
        var_dump("Now it's time to return to home and spend time with family.");
        return $this;
    }

    protected function sleep() {
        var_dump("Get rest so you can work tomorrow again.");
        return $this;
    }
}
```

```
34   class Man extends ManMachine {
35
36       public function commonWork() {
37           var_dump("Supervising the machines and instruct them to work.");
38           return $this;
39       }
40   }
41
42   class Machine extends ManMachine{
43
44       public function commonWork() {
45           var_dump("Take instruction and work accordingly.");
46           return $this;
47       }
48   }
```

Both the classes "Man" and "Machine" extend the methods of the abstract class "ManMachine". They only override the 'commonWork()' method and define it according to their own status.

Relationships between Classes

You've seen some instance of interactions between classes and objects. In software application classes and objects are related to each other. One class and its object react with other classes and objects. So we can conclude that they have relationships and that relationship depends on how one object sends message and how another object receives that message.

You can consider four different classes and objects and think about their relationships.

A truck is a kind of automobile. A car is another kind of automobile. An engine is a part of an automobile. A driver drives an automobile.

A carnivorous is an animal. The herbivorous is also an animal. They both eat. So they share a common trait – food habits.

Inheritance is another important feature of object oriented programming. It also talks about relationship. The relationship between parent class and child class can be beautifully described by the following example where a parent class first allows the derived class to go down and only after that it goes down itself.

```php
1   <?php
2
3   class Base {
4
5       public function __construct() {
6           var_dump("I am base class.");
7       }
8       public function __destruct() {
9           var_dump("The base class is going down.");
10      }
11  }
12
13  class Derived extends Base {
14
15      public function __construct() {
16          var_dump("I am derived class.");
17      }
18      public function __destruct() {
19          var_dump("The derived class is going down.");
20      }
21  }
```

```
22
23  $base = new Base();
24  $derived = new Derived();
```

Here constructors are called base to derived but the destructors cannot be controlled by the programmer. If you run this code, the output will be:

```
1  string(16) "I am base class."
2  string(19) "I am derived class."
3  string(32) "The derived class is going down."
4  string(29) "The base class is going down."
```

Relationship between classes can also be controlled by abstract classes and interfaces. Actually they allow you to practice polymorphism. Polymorphism is a kind of execution. You execute differently in response to the same message.

When we talk about food habits of carnivorous and herbivorous we actually execute them differently. Consider this code.

```
1   <?php
2
3   abstract class Animal {
4       protected abstract function FoodHabits();
5   }
6
7   class Carnivorous extends Animal {
8
9       public function FoodHabits(){
10
11          var_dump("The Carnivorous animals eat only meat.");
12
13      }
14
15  }
16
17  class Herbivorous extends Animal {
18
19      public function FoodHabits(){
20
21          var_dump("The Herbivorous animals eat only plants.");
22
23      }
```

```
24
25  }
26
27  class Implant {
28
29      public $animal;
30
31      public function FoodHabits(Animal $animal) {
32          $this->animal = $animal;
33          $this->animal->FoodHabits();
34      }
35
36  }
37
38  $implant = new Implant();
39  $carni = new Carnivorous();
40  $herbi = new Herbivorous();
41  $implant-> FoodHabits ($carni);
42  $implant-> FoodHabits ($herbi);
```

The output is quite obvious and needs no explanation any more. It's a perfect case of polymorphism. When we implement or call the food habit function it executes differently.

```
1  string(38) "The Carnivorous animals eat only meat."
2  string(40) "The Herbivorous animals eat only plants."
```

Now we can imagine a more realistic scenario where we can talk about two different authorization providers – twitter and facebook.

Consider this code:

```
1  <?php
2
3  abstract class Provider {
4      protected abstract function authorize();
5  }
6
7  class Twitter extends Provider {
8
9      public function authorize(){
10
11          var_dump("We authorize through twitter API.");
```

```
12
13        }
14
15    }
16
17    class Facebook extends Provider {
18
19        public function authorize(){
20
21            var_dump("We authorize through facebook API.");
22
23        }
24
25    }
26
27    class Login {
28
29        public $login;
30
31        public function __construct(Provider $provider) {
32            $this->login = $provider;
33            $this->login->authorize();
34        }
35
36    }
37
38    $twitter = new Twitter();
39    $facebook = new Facebook();
40    $login = new Login($twitter);
41    $login = new Login($facebook);
```

And this output:

```
1    string(33) "We authorize through twitter API."
2    string(34) "We authorize through facebook API."
```

Here polymorphism has been implemented through virtual abstract method. You can say it a kind of partial class implementation through an interface. However, there are differences between these two mechanisms of practicing polymorphism.

In the abstract class you have a virtual abstract function that you have to override in your derived class. This is also called dynamic polymorphism.

Now consider the same code this way:

```php
1    <?php
2
3    interface Provider {
4        public function authorize();
5    }
6
7    class Twitter implements Provider {
8
9        public function authorize(){
10
11            var_dump("We authorize through twitter API.");
12
13        }
14
15    }
16
17   class Facebook implements Provider {
18
19        public function authorize(){
20
21            var_dump("We authorize through facebook API.");
22
23        }
24
25    }
26
27   class Login {
28
29        public $login;
30
31        public function __construct(Provider $provider) {
32            $this->login = $provider;
33            $this->login->authorize();
34        }
35
36    }
37
38   $twitter = new Twitter();
39   $facbook = new Facebook();
40   $login = new Login($twitter);
41   $login = new Login($facbook);
```

It gives the same output.

```
1   string(33) "We authorize through twitter API."
2   string(34) "We authorize through facebook API."
```

What is the difference between two?

We have seen the same kind of dynamic polymorphism. The main difference is: an interface consumes a very little CPU as it's an empty shell, just a bunch of names; not a class. Speed matters. Not in such short code but in an embedded device it definitely matters. But programmers are divided in this issue. Some feel abstract classes are faster because interfaces require more time to find the actual method in the corresponding classes.

There are other differences too. Let us see what they are.

An interface does not provide any code. It only says: do this way. The class that implements that interface says: okay I've done this.

An abstract class may define a method by providing a code structure. At the same time it could be a virtual abstract empty method almost behaving like an interface.

An interface does not have access modifiers. It should always have public methods. Abstract class can use access modifiers. One of the major differences is the implementation headache. If you add a new method in your interface then you must track down every class where that interface has been implemented already. You have to modify them again. In abstract class there is no such binding. You can add any method to your abstract class.

However you cannot add virtual abstract function.

Static Variables, Static Functions and Singleton Pattern

Each object has its own member variables and all the member variables have their own scopes defined by the access modifiers.

If you create an integer inside a function and call that function the integer variable is created and initialized. It's destroyed once the execution completes.

In other words, as long as the function exists the variable exists. Consider a very little example.

```php
<?php

class Life {

    public $life;

    public function __construct($life) {
        $this->life = $life;
        return $this->life;
    }

    public function __destruct() {
        var_dump("I don't exist any more.");
    }

}

$a_new_life = new Life("I exist!");

var_dump($a_new_life);

Here is the output:

object(Life)#1 (1) {
  ["life"]=>
  string(8) "I exist!"
}
string(23) "I don't exist any more."
```

```
29
30   You again call the function.
31
32   $a_new_life_again = new Life("I've come back, a new life again.");
33
34   var_dump($a_new_life_again);
```

And a new output comes out with a changed value:

```
1   object(Life)#2 (1) {
2     ["life"]=>
3     string(34) "I've come back, a new life again."
4   }
5   string(23) "I don't exist any more."
```

One thing is clear. The member variables are dynamic. Can we make it static? So that it'll retain its value all the way? Let us consider this code:

```
1    <?php
2
3    class Life {
4
5        public static $life = 1;
6
7        public function __construct() {
8            var_dump("I exist!");
9        }
10
11       public static function Existance() {
12           static::$life += 1;
13           return static::$life;
14       }
15
16       public function __destruct() {
17           var_dump("I don't exist any more.");
18       }
19
20   }
21   var_dump(Life::$life);
22   var_dump(Life::Existance());
23   $a_new_life = new Life();
24   var_dump($a_new_life->Existance());
```

```
25
26  var_dump(Life::$life);
27  var_dump(Life::Existance());
28  $a_new_life_again = new Life();
29  var_dump($a_new_life_again->Existance());
```

Now consider the output carefully.

```
1   int(1) int(1)
2   int(2)
3   string(8) "I exist!"
4   int(3)
5   int(3)
6   int(4)
7   string(8) "I exist!"
8   int(5)
9   string(23) "I don't exist any more."
10  string(23) "I don't exist any more."
```

You've made the property and function static. You've tried to grab the property first and the output is 1. It's perfect. Next you've tried to grab the function (var_dump(Life::Existance());) and it's increased by 1 so the output has come out 2. That's okay. But what's happened in the next line? You've tried to create an instance of the class and wanted to call the function:

```
1   $a_new_life = new Life();
2   var_dump($a_new_life->Existance());
```

In that case the member variable should have come out as 2. In contrast it's come out as 3. It means that the member variable has retained the last value (2) and added 1 more with it.

And now comes more fun. Consider the next lines of your code.

```
1   var_dump(Life::$life);
2   var_dump(Life::Existance());
3   $a_new_life_again = new Life();
4   var_dump($a_new_life_again->Existance());
```

You've tried to grab a new value. It should have started as 1. In contrast the next lines of output were like this:

```
1  int(3)
2  int(4)
3  string(8) "I exist!"
4  int(5)
```

...

It means, creating more than one object has not reinitialized the static variable. Unlike other member variables, only one copy of the static variable exists in the memory for all the objects of that class. And as the program runs all the objects share only one copy of the static variable in the memory. The same code will produce completely different value all together if we think aboput the member variable as dynamically. Watch this code now.

```php
1   <?php
2
3   class Life {
4
5       public $life = 1;
6
7       public function __construct() {
8           var_dump("I exist!");
9       }
10
11      public function Existance() {
12          $this->life += 1;
13          return $this->life;
14      }
15
16      public function __destruct() {
17          var_dump("I don't exist any more.");
18      }
19
20  }
21
22  $a_new_life = new Life();
23  var_dump($a_new_life->Existance());
24
25  $a_new_life_again = new Life();
26  var_dump($a_new_life_again->Existance());
```

And here is the output:

```
1  string(8) "I exist!"
2  int(2)
3  string(8) "I exist!"
4  int(2)
5  string(23) "I don't exist any more."
6  string(23) "I don't exist any more."
```

Compare this with the previous code and output and you'll understand why sometimes we need static variables. To understand the difference we can have more codes. Consider this one:

```php
1  class Calculator {
2
3      public static function add() {
4          return array_sum(func_get_args());
5      }
6      public function addition(...$num) {
7          return array_sum($num);
8      }
9  }
10
11 $implant = Calculator::add(1,2,3);
12 var_dump($implant);
13 $implant1 = new Calculator();
14 var_dump($implant1->addition(1,2,3,6));
```

And the simple output:

```
1  int(6)
2  int(12)
```

More static and dynamic code example will explain this behavior well.

```php
1  <?php
2
3  class Person {
4
5      public static $age = 1;
6
7      public function age() {
8          static::$age += 1;
9      }
```

```
10  }
11
12  $ravan = new Person();
13  $ravan->age();
14  $ravan->age();
15  var_dump(Person::$age);
16  $hirimba = new Person;
17  $hirimba->age();
18  var_dump(Person::$age);
19
20  class A_Person {
21
22      public $age = 1;
23
24      public function age() {
25          $this->age++;
26      }
27      public function return_age() {
28          return $this->age;
29      }
30  }
31
32  $ravana = new A_Person();
33  $ravana->age();
34  var_dump($ravana->return_age());
35  $hirimbaa = new A_Person;
36  $hirimbaa->age();
37  var_dump($hirimbaa->return_age()),
```

And here is the output:

```
1  //first part
2  int(3)
3  int(4)
4  //second part
5  int(2)
6  int(2)
```

Before moving to the Singleton pattern we'll have another example of static code.

```php
1   <?php
2
3   class FunctionCount {
4
5       public static $count = 0;
6
7       public function CountFunction() {
8           static::$count++;
9       }
10
11      public function NumberOfCounting() {
12          for (static::$count = 0; static::$count < 10; static::$count++){
13              static::$count;
14          }
15      }
16  }
17
18  $count = new FunctionCount();
19  $count->CountFunction();
20  $count->NumberOfCounting();
21  var_dump(FunctionCount::$count); //10
22  $new_count = new FunctionCount();
23  $new_count->CountFunction();
24  var_dump(FunctionCount::$count); //11
```

And the output is quite self explanatory.

```
1   int(10)
2   int(11)
```

There is a great debate among the developers whether the static method is good or bad. If you would dig deep you'd find that the question of good or bad is insignificant. Question is: what is the reason of using static method? Is it reasonable enough to keep the value unchanged throughout the life cycle of the program or it could break the principle of encapsulation?

In real world broken encapsulation can cause issues. The same is true for Singleton pattern. The singleton pattern is only useful in some definite cases. Make sure that you need to have a single instance of class for the entire request lifecycle in a web application. Otherwise better avoid it.

For a configuration class or an event queue you may have a global object. It's not true for all purposes. Introducing a global state breaks the principle of loose coupling. It reduces testability.

Let us see how a singleton class behaves. In the following class we make sure that no instance of a class should be generated and no class can extend it any more.

```php
1   <?php
2
3   class SingleParent
4   {
5       private static $child = 0;
6
7       public static function getChild() {
8           static::$child += 1;
9           return static::$child;
10      }
11      protected function __construct() {
12      }
13      private function __clone() {
14      }
15  }
16
17  class SingleChild extends SingleParent {
18  }
19
20  $singleParent = SingleParent::getChild();
21  var_dump($singleParent);
22  $anotherSingleParent = SingleParent::getChild();
23  var_dump($anotherSingleParent);
24  $singleParent = SingleParent::getChild();
25  var_dump($singleParent);
26
27  $singleChild = SingleChild::getChild();
28  var_dump($singleChild);
```

Whenever you try to use "SingleParent" class you have to use it statically and that starts from 1 when you're calling the function getChild(). If you call it again in the same lifecycle it will stick to that static value and gets increased.

If you want to try the child class it'll throw an error.

```
1  int(1)
2  int(2)
3  int(3)
4  PHP Fatal error:  Uncaught Error: Cannot access  property SingleChild::$child in\
5    /home/hagudu/Code/php7book1/Day5/singleton.php:8
6  Stack trace:
7  #0 /home/hagudu/Code/php7book1/Day5/singleton.php(28): SingleParent::getChild()
8  #1 {main}
9    thrown in /home/hagudu/Code/php7book1/Day5/singleton.php on line 8
```

Not only that, we've also kept the constructor method protected and made it sure that the class cannot be cloned.

You've probably noticed that static methods have also been used in generating the singleton pattern. Remember static methods are useful in some cases. If you use laravel or any other php framework you'd find that static methods have been used judiciously.

You need to apply your good judgment while using it – that's all you need to be careful about.

Day 6

Well friends, we're closing in to complete our mission. Now the sixth day has arrived and we've learned many things about object oriented programming and design patterns.

Now it's time to get a glimpse about the cool features of php 7.

We'll learn about anonymous classes and we'll also learn one of the main new features – return type declarations and how we can use strict methods.

PHP 7 is Twice Faster!

What makes php 7 special?

What drives us to write a separate book on php 7? We've last seen php 5.6 and php has come a long way to prove itself as a full fledged object oriented programming language. Then why it was needed to launch php 7?

It was because php has suddenly taken a humongous jump. The first thing is the speed. It's now twice faster than the previous version. It's incorporated few cool features. And it'll keep adding in the future.

Above all what really matters is speed.

Now php 7 uses new Zend Engine 3.0 to improve application performance almost twice faster. The performance is much better when memory consumption is considered. It will also serve more parallel users without requiring any additional hardware. PHP 7 is designed and re-factored considering today's workloads. It was really necessary considering the number of web users growing everyday.

After twelve years, since 2004, it has been the most important release in the history of php.

For that reason, it's been touted to be a revolution in the way web applications can be developed and delivered for mobile to enterprises and the cloud.

Before jumping to the experiments with new cool features of php 7 we'll quickly have a look in the store of php 7. In a nutshell we'll try to understand why it's been flaunted as a revolution in the world of web programming.

To name a few, there are plenty of features that have already been added to php 7. We're going to discuss about a few.

There is a cool feature called anonymous classes. We've so far seen named classes but a support for classes without names has been added. It's a very important addition. In the next chapter we'll see what has made this anonymous class so special. There is a new operator that has come onto the stage – spaceship operator. We'll discuss about this special operator in the next chapter.

There is nothing to be said about the twice-faster speed and low memory consumption. We've told about it already. We can add one thing to that feature – the consistent support of 64 bit architecture machines.

Till now we've seen that php has been very forgiving about the type declarations. If you change the type from integer to string it doesn't protest. Now it's passé. There are scalar type declarations which enforce parameter and return types. It's been there in languages as C# or C++.

You already assume that there are more new features waiting in the queue.

Let us start with anonymous classes.

Classes Without Names

Imagine there is no border.

Borders invite wars.

There is no border and there is no war.

Can you imagine it? It's too tough probably. But in php 7 you can now have classes without names. No name collision any more!

Let's have a very brief example with a named class first.

```php
1   <?php
2
3   class ClassWithAName {
4
5    protected $TypeOfClass;
6    protected $ObjectProperty;
7
8    public function __construct($param) {
9        $this->TypeOfClass = $param;
10   }
11
12   public function ReturningProperty( $propertyName ) {
13       $this->ObjectProperty = $propertyName;
14       return $this->ObjectProperty;
15   }
16
17  }
18
19  $NamedObject = new ClassWithAName("I an class with a name");
20  $NamedObject->ReturningProperty("I am an object from a named class");
21  var_dump($NamedObject);
```

Here is the output:

```
1    object(ClassWithAName)#1 (2) {
2      ["TypeOfClass":protected]=>
3      string(22) "I an class with a name"
4      ["ObjectProperty":protected]=>
5      string(33) "I am an object from a named class"
```

That's perfect. Now we want to have an anonymous class that extends the named class.

```
1    <?php
2
3    class ClassWithAName {
4
5        public $TypeOfClass;
6        public $ObjectProperty;
7
8         public function __construct($param) {
9             $this->TypeOfClass = $param;
10        }
11
12       }
13
14
15   var_dump(new class(10) extends ClassWithAName {
16       private $num;
17
18       public function __construct($num)
19       {
20           $this->num = $num;
21       }
22   });
23
24   First we'll see what could be the output.
25
26   object(class@anonymous)#1 (3) {
27     ["num":"class@anonymous":private]=>
28     int(10)
29     ["TypeOfClass"]=>
30     NULL
31     ["ObjectProperty"]=>
32     NULL
33   }
```

It says, the object is: object(class@anonymous). It means anonymous classes are useful when simple, one-off objects need to be created. You may find a faint similarity with singleton design pattern or static properties or methods but its usefulness is different.

You may nest more anonymous classes inside classes at one go and it might become complex in that sense. Consider another piece of code.

```php
1   <?php
2
3   class Logger {
4
5       public $message;
6
7       public function log($msg){
8           $this->message = $msg;
9           var_dump($this->message);
10      }
11  }
12
13  $utility = new Logger;
14
15  $utility->log("A new log file");
```

The output will be as expected.

```
1   string(14) "A new log file"
```

Now we can introduce an anonymous class that we can pass through the log function directly.

```php
1   <?php
2
3   class Logger {
4
5       public $message;
6
7       public function log($msg){
8           $this->message = $msg;
9           var_dump($this->message);
10      }
11  }
12
13  $utility = new Logger;
```

```
14
15  $utility->log("A new log file");
16
17  // PHP 7+ code
18  $utility->log(new class {
19      public $message = "Another new message";
20      public function log($msg){
21          $this->message = $msg;
22          var_dump($this->message);
23      }
24  });
```

Now look at the output.

```
1   string(14) "A new log file"
2   object(class@anonymous)#2 (1) {
3     ["message"]=>
4     string(19) "Another new message"
5   }
```

One-off object is needed for many purposes. But never underestimate it. PHP 7 makes this feature very powerful as you can use anonymous class as any normal class. You can pass parameters through its constructor, inherits other class, implement interface and use traits.

```
1   <?php
2
3   interface AnInterface {
4   public function ForAnonymous();
5   }
6   trait ATrait {}
7
8   class ClassWithAName {
9
10      public $TypeOfClass;
11      public $ObjectProperty;
12
13      public function __construct($param) {
14          $this->TypeOfClass = $param;
15          var_dump($this->TypeOfClass);
16      }
17
18      }
```

```
19   $AnObjectWithAName = new ClassWithAName("An Instance of a class with a name.");
20   var_dump($AnObjectWithAName);
21
22   var_dump(new class("Anonymous") extends ClassWithAName implements AnInterface {
23       public $TypeOfClass = "A Class with A name";
24       public function __construct($param) {
25           $this->TypeOfClass = $param;
26           var_dump($this->TypeOfClass);
27       }
28       public function ForAnonymous(){
29           var_dump($this->TypeOfClass);
30       }
31
32       use ATrait;
33   });
```

And the output is like this:

```
1    string(35) "An Instance of a class with a name."
2    object(ClassWithAName)#1 (2) {
3      ["TypeOfClass"]=>
4      string(35) "An Instance of a class with a name."
5      ["ObjectProperty"]=>
6      NULL
7    }
8    string(9) "Anonymous"
9    object(class@anonymous)#2 (2) {
10     ["TypeOfClass"]=>
11     string(9) "Anonymous"
12     ["ObjectProperty"]=>
13     NULL
14   }
```

Consider another example where we can control the output of an addition through the anonymous class.

```
1   <?php
2
3   class Math
4   {
5       private $num1 = 1;
6       protected $num2 = 2;
7
8       protected function MathAdd()
9       {
10          return $this->num1 + $this->num2;
11      }
12
13      public function AnonymousAddition()
14      {
15          return new class($this->num1) extends Math {
16              private $num3;
17
18              public function __construct($num1)
19              {
20                  $this->num3 = $num1;
21              }
22
23              public function AddAnonymously()
24              {
25                  return $this->num2 + $this->num3 + $this->MathAdd();
26              }
27          };
28      }
29  }
30
31  var_dump((new Math)->AnonymousAddition()->AddAnonymously());
```

The output is:

```
1   int(6)
```

Watch out this line:

```
1           return new class($this->num1) extends Math {
2   ...
```

We've passed the $num1 variable through anonymous class constructor. We can easily change it any time and the output will change along with it. Let us write this line as follows:

```
1   return new class($this->num2) extends Math {
2   ...
```

Look at the output:

```
1   int(7)
```

You've nested an anonymous class within "Math" class here through a function. But only nesting an anonymous class doesn't give you the access to the private or protected property of the "Math" class.

If you'd like to get the access to the "Math" class' protected properties you should extend the "Math" class.

If you'd want to get the access to the "Math" class' private property you should pass it through its constructor.

Finally we'll see whether the anonymous class has a name or not.

First the code:

```
1   <?php
2   echo get_class(new class {});
```

And here is the output:

```
1   class@anonymous/home/hagudu/Code/php7book1/Day6/anon4.php0x7ff9b4b74022
```

This name has been given by the php engine. It basically reads the total path of the code and added a random number with it.

If you want to see that code more distinctly you can use var_dump() method.

The output will be:

```
1   string(72) class@anonymous/home/hagudu/Code/php7book1/Day6/anon4.php0x7ff4b04350\
2   45
```

So it really doesn't depend on naming. The anonymous classes are assigned names by the php engine itself. And it's done internally.

The objective is very clear.

You use it only when you need a simple, one-off object.

Know Your Type

New php 7 has come up with a very cool feature – type hinting the scalar types. You may think of them as primitive types like integers, or Booleans. And now you can set a restriction in your code and make it sure that the type you are mentioning should be followed while coding.

Consider this code:

```php
<?php

interface SetAge {
    public function setAge(int $age);
}

class Age implements SetAge {

    protected $age;
    public function setAge(int $age) {
        $this->age = $age;
        return $this->age;
    }
}

$bill = new Age();
var_dump($bill->setAge("bill"));
```

Beforehand, you could have passed any value and php was forgiving enough to have overlooked the type you were passing.

Instead of your age you could have passed your name. To catch that discrepancy you must have had a filtering system.

Now the necessity of filtering or validating your code has not diminished but at least you can have a primary guard set before you progress to the next point. Now you can use type hinting to force a function to get an argument of that type Object.

Now you can set your "age" as an integer. Watch this part of the code.

```
1   public function setAge(int $age);
2   ...
3   public function setAge(int $age) {
4           $this->age = $age;
5           return $this->age;
6       }
7   ...
```

Let us see the output first.

```
1   PHP Fatal error:  Uncaught TypeError: Argument 1 passed to Age::setAge() must be\
2    of the type integer, string given, called in /home/hagudu/Code/php7book1/Day6/s\
3   calartype.php on line 17 and defined in /home/hagudu/Code/php7book1/Day6/scalart\
4   ype.php:10
5   Stack trace:
6   #0 /home/hagudu/Code/php7book1/Day6/scalartype.php(17): Age->setAge('bill')
7   #1 {main}
8     thrown in /home/hagudu/Code/php7book1/Day6/scalartype.php on line 10
```

You were supposed to pass an integer. Instead you have passed a string. And the output says: Uncaught TypeError: Argument 1 passed to Age::setAge() must be of the type integer.

Now we'll not change the argument. We'll pass an integer like this:

```
1   var_dump($bill->setAge(10));
```

This time there is no error. It's perfect.

```
1   int(10)
```

From php 5 onwards type hinting has started been called type declarations. Consider another example.

```php
1   <?php
2
3   class Base {}
4   class Derived extends Base {}
5
6   class Outsider {}
7
8   function func(Base $base) {
9       echo get_class($base)."\n";
10  }
11
12  func(new Base);
13  func(new Derived);
14  func(new Outsider);
```

You may guess the output. It'd give an error at the end. The first two lines are perfect and smooth running. But in thest line there is a glitch.

Your type hinting or declarations didn't allow the function to require the object of "Base" class. It was an object of the "Outsider" class which didn't have any relationships with the "Base" or "Derived" class. It expected parameters of certain types. The expectations didn't match.

Look at the output:

```
1   Base
2   Derived
3   PHP Fatal error:  Uncaught TypeError: Argument 1 passed to func() must be an ins\
4   tance of Base, instance of Outsider given, called in /home/hagudu/Code/php7book1\
5   /Day6/typehint.php on line 14 and defined in /home/hagudu/Code/php7book1/Day6/ty\
6   pehint.php:8
7   Stack trace:
8   #0 /home/hagudu/Code/php7book1/Day6/typehint.php(14): func(Object(Outsider))
9   #1 {main}
10    thrown in /home/hagudu/Code/php7book1/Day6/typehint.php on line 8
```

First two lines are perfect. But the next line says: Uncaught TypeError: Argument 1 passed to func() must be an instance of Base, instance of Outsider given.

Since the given value was of the incorrect type, an error was generated. In PHP 5, this is normally a recoverable fatal error. From PHP 7 it throws a TypeError exception.

For interfaces or contracts the same rule applies.

```php
1   <?php
2   interface Contract { public function func(); }
3   class Base implements Contract { public function func() {} }
4
5   // This doesn't implement the interface.
6   class Outsider {}
7
8   function newFunction(Contract $contract) {
9       echo get_class($contract)."\n";
10  }
11
12  newFunction(new Base);
13  newFunction(new Outsider);
```

It will throw a type error as before.

```
1   Base
2   PHP Fatal error:  Uncaught TypeError: Argument 1 passed to newFunction() must im\
3   plement interface Contract, instance of Outsider given, called in /home/hagudu/C\
4   ode/php7book1/Day6/typehint.php on line 27 and defined in /home/hagudu/Code/php7\
5   book1/Day6/typehint.php:22
6   Stack trace:
7   #0 /home/hagudu/Code/php7book1/Day6/typehint.php(27): newFunction(Object(Outside\
8   r))
9   #1 {main}
10    thrown in /home/hagudu/Code/php7book1/Day6/typehint.php on line 22
```

Remember few things. When you specify a type declaration, the type name should be added before the parameter name.

Can we make it more Strict?

We know that php is extremely fohiving. By default it coerces values of the wrong type into the expected type if possible.

We've seen different scenes in the earlier phase of PHP. If a function expects an integer for a parameter and is given a string instead, it normally tries to translate that to a type string.

Now we can apply more strict rules. So that if a function expects an integer, you have to give it an integer or it will throw a type error. You can enable strict mode per file basis.

First let us consider the weak typing example.

```
1  function add( int $a, int $b) {
2      return $a + $b;
3  }
4
5  var_dump(add(1, 2));
6  var_dump(add(1.5, 2.5));
```

This is not an exception that in weak-typing code an integer may be given to a function which is actually expecting a float. In that case, it'll be coerced to integers. Watch the output.

```
1  int(3)
2  int(3)
```

Now we're going to apply more strict rules. Watch this code.

```
1  <?php
2
3  declare(strict_types=1);
4
5  function sum( int $a, int $b) {
6      return $a + $b;
7  }
8
9  var_dump(sum(1, 2));
10 var_dump(sum(1.5, 2.5));
```

We've used declare() function and said that strict types should be applied. And after that we're trying to pass floating values in place of integers. The expected fall out should have been a type error.

Let us watch the output.

```
1  int(3)
2  PHP Fatal error:  Uncaught TypeError: Argument 1 passed to sum() must be of the \
3  type integer, float given, called in /home/hagudu/Code/php7book1/Day6/stricttype\
4  .php on line 10 and defined in /home/hagudu/Code/php7book1/Day6/stricttype.php:5
5  Stack trace:
6  #0 /home/hagudu/Code/php7book1/Day6/stricttype.php(10): sum(1.5, 2.5)
7  #1 {main}
8    thrown in /home/hagudu/Code/php7book1/Day6/stricttype.php on line 5
```

Remember if you enable strict mode, the declare statement is used with the strict_types declaration. And the strict type mode affects the return type declarations.

Return Type Declarations

This feature has been added in PHP 7. Return type declarations specify the type of the value that will be returned from a function. It's similar to the argument type declarations.

It's quite natural that in the weak mode php will try to translate the return value as far as possible. It'll be coerced in the new value.

If strict method is applied the return value should be of correct type. Let us consider a normal class declaration where we create a new person object.

```php
1   <?php
2
3   class Person {
4       protected $person;
5       public function __construct($person) {
6           return $this->person = $person;
7       }
8   }
9
10  var_dump(new Person("Bill"));
```

The output is quite normal.

```
1   object(Person)#1 (1) {
2     ["person":protected]=>
3     string(4) "Bill"
4   }
```

Let us change the previous code into this:

```php
1   <?php
2
3   class Person {
4       protected $person;
5       public function __construct($person) {
6           return $this->person = $person;
7       }
8   }
9
10  function GetPerson () {
11      return new Person("Bill");
```

```
12  }
13
14  var_dump(GetPerson());
```

This code remains in weak mode. We have no way to stop the default forceful method to adapt this code to return something else. Normally it gives this output lke it's given before.

```
1  object(Person)#1 (1) {
2    ["person":protected]=>
3    string(4) "Bill"
4  }
```

What happens if we change this part of code?

```
1  <?php
2
3  class Person {
4      protected $person;
5      public function __construct($person) {
6          return $this->person = $person;
7      }
8  }
9  function GetPerson () {
10     //return new Person("Bill");
11     return [];
12 }
13
14 var_dump(GetPerson());
```

It'll give the output – array - as expected.

```
1  array(0) {
2  }
```

It means no strict type has been in place so php has tried to translate it.

Now we'll apply the strict type this way.

```php
1   <?php
2
3   class Person {
4       protected $person;
5       public function __construct($person) {
6           return $this->person = $person;
7       }
8   }
9
10  function GetPerson () : Person {
11      return new Person("Bill");
12  }
13
14  var_dump(GetPerson());
```

The output is as expected as we have tried to return correct type:

```
1   object(Person)#1 (1) {
2     ["person":protected]=>
3     string(4) "Bill"
4   }
```

Now change this code to return an incorrect type.

```php
1   <?php
2
3   class Person {
4       protected $person;
5       public function __construct($person) {
6           return $this->person = $person;
7       }
8   }
9
10  function GetPerson () : Person {
11      //return new Person("Bill");
12      return [];
13  }
14
15  var_dump(GetPerson());
```

What'll be the output? We have tried to return an array instead of a person instance.

Look at the output:

```
1  PHP Fatal error:  Uncaught TypeError: Return value of GetPerson() must be an ins\
2  tance of Person, array returned in /home/hagudu/Code/php7book1/Day6/returntype.p\
3  hp:12
4  Stack trace:
5  #0 /home/hagudu/Code/php7book1/Day6/returntype.php(15): GetPerson()
6  #1 {main}
7    thrown in /home/hagudu/Code/php7book1/Day6/returntype.php on line 12
```

It expectedly says, "Uncaught TypeError: Return value of GetPerson() must be an instance of Person, array returned...". We can extend this code in a stricter way.

```
1  class Person {}
2
3  interface LogInterface {
4      public function Log() : Person;
5  }
6
7  class Loggingin implements LogInterface {
8      public function Log() : Person {
9          return new Person;
10     }
11 }
12
13 $login = new Loggingin();
14 var_dump($login->Log());
```

The output is expected.

```
1  object(Person)#2 (0) {
2  }
```

If you try to return an incorrect type what happens?

```
1  class Logingin implements LogInterface {
2      public function Log() : Person {
3          //return new Person;
4          return [];
5      }
6  }
```

There will be a type error as expected.

```
 1  PHP Fatal error:  Uncaught TypeError: Return value of Logingin::Log() must be an\
 2   instance of Person, array returned in          /home/hagudu/Code/php7book1/Day6/mo\
 3  rereturntype.php:12
 4
 5  Stack trace:
 6
 7  #0 /home/hagudu/Code/php7book1/Day6/morereturntype.php(17): Logingin->Log()
 8
 9  #1 {main}
10
11    thrown in /home/hagudu/Code/php7book1/Day6/morereturntype.php on line 12
```

In the "LogInterface" we expect that a new user will log in. It's not mandatory that since php 7 supports strict type you've to use that. But if you do it it'd be always better since the contract is expecting a genuine user instance, not an array or any incorrect type.

Day 7

We are nearing to the end of our mission. Each day, painstakingly, we've learned how to code in object oriented way.

We've learned what major design patterns in php are and finally we're learning the cool new features of php 7.

These final chapters will not take your time. It'll be smaller and faster than the previous ones.

You're about to touch the finishing line!

Group 'Use' Declarations

In php 7, you could use namespace in a different way. Suppose in our root folder we have a folder called "Day7". In that folder you've kept two files – 'groupclasses.php' and 'index.php'.

Now you've decided to keep 'groupclasses.php' under namespace "PHP7BOOK".

And under that namespace you keep two classes – Person and Animal.

The code is simple.

```php
1   <?php namespace PHP7BOOK;
2
3   class Person {}
4   class Animal {}
```

Now in the same folder you also keep 'index.php' and decide to create instances of Person and Animal in that file.

What'll you do?

Very simple. Either you can call those class directly this way.

```php
1   <?php
2   require 'groupclasses.php';
3
4   var_dump(new PHP7BOOK\Person);
5   var_dump(new PHP7BOOK\Animal());
6
7   If you run the code it'll give this output:
8
9   object(PHP7BOOK\Person)#1 (0) {
10  }
11  object(PHP7BOOK\Animal)#1 (0) {
12  }
```

Pretty simple staff. You could have written the same code in this style also.

```php
<?php
require 'groupclasses.php';
use PHP7BOOK\Person;
use PHP7BOOK\Animal;
var_dump(new Person());
var_dump(new Animal());
```

And you get the same effect in your output.

In php 7 you can use classes, functions and constants in a new way. It can be imported from the same namespace and it can now be grouped together in a single use statement.

```php
use PHP7BOOK\{Animal, Person};
var_dump(new Animal());
var_dump(new Person());
```

It reduces the lines of codes. And, besides, it also maximizes the readability.

Our Spaceship

<⇒

Oh, what is this?

Is it a spaceship?

Yes, it looks like a modern spaceship and the creator may have thought the name for that reason. This new feature is called spaceship operator.

What does it do?

Let us assume a "cart" object in an e-commerce portal. It's not related to php 7. We write down a simple array.

```php
1   <?php
2
3   /*
4    * The spaceship operator in php 7
5    */
6
7   $cart = ["Book", "Shoe", "Watch", "TV", "Mobile", "Perfume"];
8
9   sort($cart);
10
11  var_dump($cart);
```

We have sorted it out so the output comes out as this – alphabetically orderd.

```
1   array(6) {
2     [0]=>
3     string(4) "Book"
4     [1]=>
5     string(6) "Mobile"
6     [2]=>
7     string(7) "Perfume"
8     [3]=>
9     string(4) "Shoe"
10    [4]=>
11    string(2) "TV"
```

```
12    [5]=>
13    string(5) "Watch"
14  }
```

If we reverse it the output will be reversed. There should not be any problem regarding this.

PHP 7 has thought about it in a new way.

Can we change the order or compare the items in the run time with the help of a call back function?

Let us show the code first. Then we'll have an explanation how it happens.

Let us write the same code this way:

```php
1   <?php
2
3   /*
4    * The spaceship operator in php 7
5    */
6
7   $cart = ["Book", "Shoe", "Watch", "TV", "Mobile", "Perfume"];
8   usort($cart, function($item1, $item2) {
9       var_dump("ITEM1 : " . $item1 . " ITEM2 : " . $item2);
10  });
11
12  var_dump($cart);
```

We're curious about seeing the comparison between the items. So we have 'var_dump()' them.

Let us see the output first.

```
1   string(25) "ITEM1 : Book ITEM2 : Shoe"
2   string(26) "ITEM1 : Shoe ITEM2 : Watch"
3   string(24) "ITEM1 : Watch ITEM2 : TV"
4   string(25) "ITEM1 : TV ITEM2 : Mobile"
5   string(30) "ITEM1 : Mobile ITEM2 : Perfume"
6   array(6) {
7     [0]=>
8     string(4) "Book"
9     [1]=>
10    string(4) "Shoe"
11    [2]=>
12    string(5) "Watch"
13    [3]=>
14    string(2) "TV"
```

```
15    [4]=>
16    string(6) "Mobile"
17    [5]=>
18    string(7) "Perfume"
19  }
```

We've expected it so nothing new in it.

Can we compare their length mow?

Let us write this code using spaceship operator.

```
1   <?php
2
3   /*
4    * The spaceship operator in php 7
5    */
6
7   $cart = ["Book", "Shoe", "Watch", "TV", "Mobile", "Perfume"];
8   usort($cart, function($item1, $item2) {
9       return strlen($item1) <=> strlen($item2);
10  });
11
12  var_dump($cart);
```

As of now you just think that we're comparing the lengths of the items. We've just seen in the previous code how item 1 has been compared with item 2.

Keeping that in mind, let us look at the output first.

```
1   array(6) {
2     [0]=>
3     string(2) "TV"
4     [1]=>
5     string(4) "Book"
6     [2]=>
7     string(4) "Shoe"
8     [3]=>
9     string(5) "Watch"
10    [4]=>
11    string(6) "Mobile"
12    [5]=>
13    string(7) "Perfume"
14  }
```

It clearly shows how it comes out in an ordered way according to the lengths of the items.

Question is how it happens?

Let us think this way?

When we compare the values of two variables it first checks whether the value of the first variable is less than the second one. Next it checks whether it's equal. And finally it checks whether it's greater.

If it comes out that the first value is less then it's represented as -1. It they are equal then the value is 0. Finally if the first one is greater then the value is 1.

It means: 1<⇒1 comes out as 0.

Consider this code.

```php
<?php
// Integers
echo 1 <=> 1;
echo 1 <=> 2;
echo 2 <=> 1;
```

And the output will be.

```
0
-1
1
```

In case of strings it always checks the position of the alphabetical orders. That means "a" is always less than "b".

Other few features

Let us check few other cool features of php 7. It's quite natural by the time book finally comes out there should have been more features added to to php 7. Please chack the documentation page and try to remain updated.

Closure::call()

Before php 7 comes, we need to use 'bindto()' function as intermediate closure.

Consider this code before php 7.

```php
<?php

class SomeClass {
    private $variable = 1;
}

$getVariableThroughBinding = function() {
    return $this->x;
};
$getVariable = $getVariableThroughBinding->bindTo(new SomeClass(), 'SomeClass');\
// intermediate closure
var_dump($getVariable);
```

And the output is as expected.

```
object(Closure)#3 (1) {
  ["this"]=>
  object(SomeClass)#2 (1) {
    ["variable":"SomeClass":private]=>
    int(1)
  }
}
```

PHP 7 has changed this scenario completely.

Now you can bind an object scope to a closure in a much shorter way.

```php
1   <?php
2
3   class SomeClass {
4       private $variable = 1;
5   }
6   $getVariable = function() {
7       return $this->variable;
8   };
9   var_dump($getVariable->call(new SomeClass()));
```

It gives us same output.

Integer division with intdiv()

A new function 'intdiv()' has been inducted into php 7.

It's a simple method to return an integer by divdiding the operands.

Let us see a simple example.

```php
1   var_dump(intdiv(1105.55, 3.2));
```

It returns an integer 368.

Null coalescing operator

Let us consider a code of chacking the age first. It checks whether the 'age' is given in the form or not. If it's not given, then it says 'not mentioned'. When it's given it just spits out the age. Very basic thing we normally did when php 7 had not come.

```php
1   <?php
2   $age = isset($_GET['age']) ? $_GET['age'] : 'not mentioned';
3
4   var_dump($age);
```

As usual it'll give an output of – 'not mentioned.' Now we write this code with the age given.

```php
1   <?php
2
3   $_GET['age'] = 10;
4
5   $age = isset($_GET['age']) ? $_GET['age'] : 'not mentioned';
6
7   var_dump($age);
```

As expected it gives us the age now, which is 10. But php 7 has made it more simple and fun to train the gun in a really simple way. No more you have to chack whether the variable value is set ot not. We can write the same code in a more simple way.

```php
1   $age = $_GET['age'] ?? 'not mentioned';
2   var_dump($age);
```

Run the code and the output is:

```
1   string(13) "not mentioned"
```

And provide the value you'll get the value right away. It's so simple.

Epilogue: What Next

Well, we have walked a long way together. But, my dear friend, there is a longer way lies ahead infront of us.

From now on I hope you'll find coding a beautiful way of living. You'll learn more new things whether you become a professional or a hobbyist. Coding teaches us to be logical and reasonable. Php 7 will come out many more new features in the future to make your coding experience more fruitful and it'll be a real fun to do something new.

Read the documentation and try to do something new.

If you want to catch me there are several options open before you.

You can mail me at: *sanjib12sinha@gmail.com*

You can tweet me to: *@sanjibsinha*

Feel free to ask any question and send your feedback.

Best wishes.

Printed in Great Britain
by Amazon